DETAINED, DENIED, DEPORTED

ASYLUM SEEKERS IN THE UNITED STATES

A HELSINKI WATCH REPORT

DETAINED, DENIED, DEPORTED:

ASYLUM SEEKERS IN THE UNITED STATES

Helsinki Watch

June 1989

© 1989 by the U.S. Helsinki Watch Committee
All rights reserved
Printed in the United States of America
ISBN 0-929692-22-5
Cover Design: Deborah Thomas

U.S. HELSINKI WATCH COMMITTEE

The U.S. Helsinki Watch Committee is a nongovernmental organization founded in 1979 to promote domestic and international compliance with the human rights provisions of the 1975 Helsinki accords. The Chairman of Helsinki Watch is Robert L. Bernstein; Vice Chairwoman, Alice A. Henkin; Executive Director, Jeri Laber; Research Director, Catherine A. Fitzpatrick; Research Associate, Janet Fleischman; Consultant, Lois Whitman; Assistant to the Executive Director, Nancy Beatty; Assistant, Mia Nitchun; Intern, Karin König.

HUMAN RIGHTS WATCH

Human Rights Watch is composed of five Watch Committees:

Americas Watch, Africa Watch, Asia Watch, Helsinki Watch and Middle East Watch.

Executive Committee: Robert L. Bernstein (Chairman); Adrian W. DeWind (Vice Chairman); Roland Algrant; Dorothy Cullman; Jack Greenberg; Alice A. Henkin; Stephen Kass; Jeri Laber; Aryeh Neier; Matthew Nimetz; Bruce Rabb; Kenneth Roth.

Staff: Executive Director, Aryeh Neier; Deputy Director, Kenneth Roth; Washington Director, Holly J. Burkhalter; Press Director, Susan Osnos; Research Associate, Joanna Weschler.

TABLE OF CONTENTS

ACKNOWLEDGMENTS i
INTRODUCTION 1
SUMMARY 3
RECOMMENDATIONS 7
THE INTERNATIONAL STANDARDS OF
   REFUGEE PROTECTION 9
HISTORICAL ORIENTATION OF THE
   U.S. ASYLUM SITUATION 13
U.S. ASYLUM: PROCEDURES AND CRITERIA 17
   General 17
      The Law 17
      The Authorities Involved 17
      The Steps of the Procedure 17
   Methods of Obtaining Political Asylum in the U.S. 18
      Applying With an INS District Director 19
      Applying With an Immigration Judge 21
      Appealing Decisions of Immigration Judges 21
      The Criteria for Decisions on Asylum and
         Withholding of Deportation 23
         Significance of Civil War or Severe
            Disturbances of Public Order 26
         Alternative Refuge Within the Country of
            Persecution 29
      Level of Evidence 29
      Discretionary Denial of Asylum 30
      Status of Asylum Seekers During Proceedings 34
      Status of Asylum Seekers After a Final Decision 34
      Recent Legal Developments 35

Methods of Obtaining Refugee Status in the
  Overseas Admission Process: 38

U.S. ASYLUM: POLICIES AND PRACTICES 45

  Detention 45
  Interdiction of Haitians 50
  Other Deterrence Practices 55
    INS Treatment of Central American Asylum Seekers 55
    New INS Policy Towards Central American Asylum Seekers . . 59
    Biases Due to Foreign Policy Interests 63
    Work Authorization 66
    Right to Counsel 68
  The Role of the State Department Advisory Opinions 69

THE NEED FOR TEMPORARY PROTECTION 75

APPENDICES 79

SOURCES 85

ACKNOWLEDGMENTS

This report was written by Karin König, a lawyer and intern with Helsinki Watch under the International Human Rights Internship Program administered by the International Institute of Education, Washington D.C., and funded by the Raoul Wallenberg Committee, New York City.

It is based on interviews conducted with and information provided by members of various refugee advocacy groups, immigration attorneys and activists in the field of refugee protection. Research materials include documents on individual asylum cases and a variety of studies, articles and administrative and judicial decisions listed at the end of the report.

Helsinki Watch gratefully acknowledges the invaluable assistance provided by Arthur C. Helton, Director of the Political Asylum Project of the Lawyers Committee for Human Rights, New York City. Helsinki Watch is also indebted to Anne Fuller, Assistant Director of the National Coalition for Haitian Refugees; Sr. Rosemarie Jefferson, Southside Community Mission Annex, Immigration and Refugee Service, Brooklyn; CARECEN (Central American Refugee Center), Hempstead (Long Island) and Los Angeles; and Jeffrey Heller and Claudia Slovinsky, attorneys at law in New York City.

INTRODUCTION

The task that states have taken on in granting refuge in the form of asylum to persons fleeing persecution and general conditions of violence and upheaval is a deeply humanitarian one that has little-by-little become part of international law. Although the right to asylum is not yet recognized by the international community to be one of the basic human rights, the need for it stems from a lack of respect by governments for internationally-recognized human rights.

Wars, civil strife, often resulting in famines, and totalitarian regimes are largely responsible for the fact that people flee their homelands, often under very dangerous circumstances. The decision to take this step results in grave consequences for refugees, making them more vulnerable than other foreigners and immigrants and, thus, more in need of protection.

The states where these people seek refuge have a moral and legal obligation at least to grant them refuge by not sending them back to the country where their lives or freedom were threatened. Because the majority of all refugees worldwide seek refuge in neighboring countries, or countries on the same continent, the overwhelming share of the international responsibility to provide asylum to refugees is being fulfilled by countries that are among the poorest of the world, such as Malawi and Pakistan.

At the same time, some of the wealthiest countries of the world, such as the United States, Canada and countries of Western Europe, argue that they are overwhelmed by asylum seekers. By claiming that the majority of them are not refugees but "economic migrants" fleeing poverty and underdevelopment and "abusing" the asylum system, the governments of these countries seek to justify the introduction of restrictive policies and deterrence measures that violate international as well as national refugee law. This attitude is based on the assumption that the distinction between refugees and economic migrants is a sharp one. In fact, political and economic reasons for fleeing countries are increasingly mixed.

Numerous U.S. experts in the field of asylum and refugee law charge that U.S. asylum and refugee practices and policies have failed to comply with international refugee standards, as set by the Refugee Convention, as well as with domestic standards, as set by the Refugee Act, enacted by Congress in 1980 with the intent to eliminate previous political and geographical bias.

Concerned about these threats to refugee protection, Helsinki Watch decided to look into the situation in the United States in terms of compliance with national law and with international humanitarian and human rights standards. We are aware that there are a considerable number of unwarranted applications for political asylum in the U.S. Yet many applicants who do not meet the narrow refugee criteria, sometimes because of a narrow interpretation by the authorities in charge, still do have *bona fide* claims. In human rights terms as well as those of internationally recognized principles of refugee protection, it is essential that the U.S. government guarantee and ensure free access to fair refugee determination proceedings in the U.S. in order to determine whether asylum applicants meet the required criteria. Sweeping restrictive measures endanger genuine refugees.

Helsinki Watch advocates the continuation of a generous and humane asylum and refugee policy by the U.S. toward all nationalities. We are convinced that it is in the best interests of the United States to resume leadership in the field of refugee protection. By examining U.S. law, recent administrative and jurisdictional developments in the refugee determination process, and policies that have been heavily criticized by refugee advocacy groups, this report seeks to raise public awareness of recent threats to the system of refugee protection in the United States and to enlist public support for a better system.

SUMMARY

"I cannot believe that this nation with such a high regard for human dignity will turn us away." Juan Calero, 26, refugee from Nicaragua, facing deportation under new U.S. government policies in Texas.*

After World War II, the United States made a significant contribution to developing an international system of refugee protection and was an outstanding example in providing refuge to many coming to its borders in desperate search for a safe haven. The country's traditional role as an asylum giver, however, has been undermined in recent years by practices aimed at deterring refugees, especially those from Central America and Haiti, from coming to the United States without valid travel documents, including those who intend to apply for political asylum. These deterrence measures have prevented asylum seekers from using the procedures that national law accords them. They are eroding the system of protection for refugees in the United States, and may also exert a negative influence on other countries.

Deterrence measures affect refugees on several levels. Practices such as the Haitian Interdiction Program, the setting of low annual ceilings for certain areas, and the designation of only Communist or leftist countries in these areas for the Overseas Refugee Admission Process prevent refugees or asylum seekers from entering the United States at all. Measures such as long-term detention and inhumane treatment in detention facilities, restrictions of the movement of asylum seekers (as they have recently been introduced by the Immigration and Naturalization Service (INS) in the Rio Grande Valley in Texas where most Central American refugees enter the U.S.), denial of a fair asylum determination process, and denial of work permits are designed to and do often

---

* The New York Times, February 27, 1989, "Aliens Say New Curbs Won't Halt Them at Border."

succeed in discouraging refugees from applying for asylum or from appealing negative decisions. Often they are forced to return to their countries while others are deterred from coming.

These measures do not only make a mockery of the spirit of national and international refugee law but also directly violate the Refugee Act and the U.N. Refugee Convention. Insofar as they are designed to or succeed in preventing refugees from applying for asylum or appealing negative decisions, they violate the statutory right to apply for asylum. To the extent that they prevent them from coming to the country or make them return to countries where their lives or freedom may be threatened, they violate the non-refoulement principle according to the U.N. Refugee Convention. Furthermore, INS detention policy violates the right not be deprived of one's liberty without due process according to the U.S. Constitution and international human rights instruments.

The enactment of the Refugee Act in 1980 was designed by Congress to eliminate former political and geographical bias towards certain groups of refugees and asylum seekers. However, U.S. asylum and refugee practices and policies have continued to be politicized and ideologically motivated. Asylum statistics and figures for both annual regional ceilings and actual admission of refugees in the overseas admission process clearly reflect a double standard.

There is an important institutional component to the Justice Department's failure to implement the Refugee Act. The authority in charge of the proceedings, the Immigration and Naturalization Service, is primarily concerned with immigration law enforcement. As part of the executive branch, it is strongly influenced by the government's immigration and foreign policy concerns. Asylum related activities represent only a small portion of its overall institutional mandate. All this has contributed to the fact that the INS treats asylum seekers, especially in cases of mass influx, in inhumane and illegal ways; that INS examiners and district directors tend to interpret asylum laws as restrictively as possible; that they require applicants to meet an unrealistic level of evidence and fail to implement liberal decisions by administrative and judicial bodies in defining refugees.

An additional factor is that INS officials and immigration judges adjudicating asylum claims lack any special training in the field and, therefore, tend to rely to a large extent on State Department advisory opinions. The State Department asylum officers in charge of issuing these opinions base their evaluation on the State Department's annual "Country Reports on Human Rights Practices" which often reflect foreign policy interests and thus introduce political bias into the process. This dependency of asylum adjudicators on politicized State Department opinions is one of the major weaknesses in the entire process and is responsible for much inconsistency and lack of credibility of the U.S. asylum procedure.

Helsinki Watch is also concerned about the administration of the Overseas Refugee Admission Process which also fails to comply with the Refugee Act. It continues to be dominated by geographical and ideological limitations. Both the designation of regional ceilings and actual admissions still favor refugees from Communist and leftist countries and exclude refugees from countries torn by civil strife whose governments have a friendly relationship with the U.S. government. In contradiction to the Refugee Act, it tends to be a group determination process admitting applicants from favored areas regardless of whether they individually meet the criteria of the refugee definition. While Helsinki Watch does not object in principle to generosity in the admission of applicants form certain areas, we do if the result is that applicants from other areas are subjected to more stringent admissions.

Since the enactment of the Refugee Act, the overall annual ceiling for refugee admissions has dropped dramatically to less than half the number of 1980. Given the importance of the process in terms of the number of annual refugee admissions, the procedure is poorly administered and fails to provide many applicants with an adequate and fair process to have their claims evaluated. The lack of any guarantee of due process has most recently especially affected Indochinese refugees, a large number of whom have been denied refugee status without the assistance of counsel and without having the right to appeal the decision.

Finally, aliens who do not meet the narrow criteria of the refugee definition, sometimes also due to a narrow interpretation by the U.S. authorities, but whose life or freedom would nevertheless be in danger if forced to return to their home countries do not enjoy any effective protection in the

United States. Extended Voluntary Departure, a temporary non-deportation status that is granted at the discretion of the Attorney General to nationals of certain countries in crises, is applied inconsistently. It has also favored refugees from countries that do not share an ideological interest with the U.S. government, excluding mainly refugees from Central American countries torn by civil strife, such as El Salvador and Guatemala. It is presently in effect for Afghans, Ethiopians and Poles. A legislative proposal from 1987, the Temporary Safe Haven Act, addresses the need for the generic protection of persons in refugee-like situations in an efficient way. It fails, however, to narrow adequately the Attorney General's discretion in determining the countries of origin from which refugees are to be granted relief.

RECOMMENDATIONS

Helsinki Watch calls upon the U.S. Administration to bring the treatment of refugees and asylum seekers into accordance with traditional U.S. humanitarian principles, U.S. laws and international agreements by:

1) abolishing measures that are designed to deter asylum seekers from coming to the United States, applying for asylum or appealing negative decisions, and that often force them to return to countries where their lives or freedom may be threatened. In particular, Helsinki Watch calls for an end to the Haitian Interdiction Program and the detention program directed against undocumented aliens which heavily affects asylum seekers. The detention program should be restricted to its purpose before 1980: to detain only those individuals who either constitute a threat to society or are likely to abscond;

2) ensuring that INS treatment of asylum seekers, particularly in the border areas near Central America, is in accordance with U.S. and international law by providing special training to agents in the field of adjudication of asylum claims and in evaluating conditions in the asylum seekers' countries of origin; and by specifically instructing agents to conduct fair interviews with the assistance of counsel and capable interpreters, to adjudicate employment authorization requests within the mandated time and extend work permits while asylum cases are pending.

3) eliminating political bias by reforming the U.S. asylum determination process; it is essential to involve independent organizations in the task of providing information on human rights conditions to asylum adjudicators and to shift the focus away from the State Department advisory opinions. Asylum officers and immigration judges should receive comprehensive training in the field of human rights law and conditions as well as refugee law. Ideally, an agency independent from both the Department of Justice and the Department of State should be entrusted with asylum adjudication, or such an agency should at least be involved in the procedure;

4) ensuring a generous and non-discriminatory admission of refugees from areas where agencies like the UNHCR determine a need for it; providing guarantees of due process, most importantly a formal right of appeal, to applicants in the Overseas Admission Process;

5) fully implementing decisions by administrative and judicial bodies regarding the interpretation of the refugee criteria by instructions to authorities in charge of the proceedings.

Furthermore, Helsinki Watch urges Congress to monitor implementation of the Refugee Act, passed in order to bring U.S. asylum and refugee procedures and practice into conformity with international law, and to supplement it, by:

1) taking legislative action, if necessary, to force the administration to carry out the steps recommended above;

2) enacting generic legislation for the protection of persons in refugee-like situations that sufficiently controls the Attorney General's discretion in the determination process in order to ensure consistent and impartial application.

THE INTERNATIONAL STANDARDS OF REFUGEE PROTECTION

International law is developed only minimally as far as protection of refugees is concerned. Most importantly, it establishes the right of refugees not to be forcibly returned to a country where their life or freedom may be threatened. The refugee definition of the 1951 U.N. Refugee Convention established a restrictive concept based on the type of refugees who were typical after World War II. Nearly 40 years later, this concept is highly inadequate for the majority of individuals who are escaping from situations of civil war and other forms of civil strife that are responsible to an overwhelming extent for the 13.3 million* refugees worldwide. International efforts to broaden this definition have failed so far. For these reasons, international instruments provide only a minimum standard for refugee protection.

In international law, the right of asylum refers to the right of a state to protect an alien from persecution. This means that a state granting asylum to an alien is not to be considered hostile towards the alien's country of origin or the state that persecuted the alien. This interpretation does not include, however, the right of an individual who is being persecuted to be granted asylum in another state.

The Universal Declaration of Human Rights, proclaimed by the United Nations on December 10, 1948, stipulates in Article 14 that "everyone has the right to seek and to enjoy in other countries asylum from persecution." But the United Nations (U.N.) Covenants on Civil and Political, and Economic, Cultural and Social Rights of 1966, which implement the Universal Declaration of Human Rights in the form of binding treaties, do not contain any provisions on asylum. The Declarations on Territorial Asylum by the General Assembly

---

* According to the United Nations High Commissioner for Refugees.

of the United Nations also leave it to the discretion of the contracting states as to whether or not to grant asylum to aliens in danger of persecution. Efforts to create an individual right to asylum in a universal convention, as were undertaken, for instance, at the U.N. Conference on Territorial Asylum in 1977, have failed so far. States have not been willing to accept restrictions of their power to limit immigration and to control their borders.

A number of important international standards have, however, been indirectly formulated by laws regulating the treatment and status of refugees. On July 28, 1951, the United Nations adopted the *Convention Relating to the Status of Refugees.* It applies only to persons who became refugees as a result of events that took place before January 1951. The Convention contains a definition of those persons who are considered to be refugees: Art. 1, par. 2, accords refugee status to every person

> ...who owing to a well-founded fear of being persecuted for reasons of race, religion, nationality, membership of a particular social group or political opinion, is outside the country of his nationality and is unable or, owing to such fear, is unwilling to avail himself of the protection of that country.

Many contracting countries have set up procedures for determining refugee status of aliens and provide asylum to those whom they recognize as refugees. The signatory states did not undertake, however, any obligation to grant asylum to persons meeting the definition. According to Article 33, a crucial part of the Convention, they are obliged, however, not to expel or return (refouler) a refugee

> to the frontiers of territories where his life or freedom would be threatened on account of his race, religion, nationality, membership of a particular social group or political opinion.

This provision is called the principle of non-refoulement. It is the most important international obligation regarding refugee protection. The contracting states must comply with this principle also when they are expelling or returning a refugee to a state other than the persecuting country; they must consider whether the refugee would also be persecuted there, or whether the refugee would be in danger of being expelled or returned by the third country to the country of persecution. According to traditional concepts of international law, the refugee or asylum seeker is protected by the principle of non-refoulement only if he/she is in the territory of the contracting state. In harmony with the spirit of the U.N. Refugee Convention, the term "in the territory" must be defined as broadly as possible. The principle of non-refoulement applies to whatever situation exists at the border where a refugee is to be refused admittance or returned.

The U.N. Refugee Convention also lays down a minimum standard for the treatment of refugees. The signatory states shall apply the provisions of the Convention without discrimination as to race, religion or country of origin. According to Article 31 of the Convention Relating to the Status of Refugees, the treatment of refugees who have entered the country illegally, or are in the country illegally, shall live up to a minimum standard. No penalties, on account of their illegal entry or presence, shall be imposed on such refugees, and no unnecessary restrictions shall be applied to their movements.

In 1951, the United Nations established the office of the *High Commissioner for Refugees (UNHCR)* and assigned it a special responsibility to provide refugees with legal and material protection. There are representatives of the High Commissioner in many contracting countries. UNHCR generally monitors the implementation of the United Nations refugee instruments by the signatory states and developments in the countries with regard to the guidelines, as they are set forth in the Handbook on Procedures and Criteria for Determining Refugee Status of 1979.

The role and influence of the representatives of the High Commissioner in the procedures for determining refugee status and granting asylum varies considerably from country to country according to national legislation. They may maintain a formal role in the procedure by being entitled to participate in the decision-making process, as is, for instance, the case in the Netherlands, or they may not be formally involved at all, as is the case in the United States.

The *Protocol Relating to the Status of Refugees,* adopted by the United Nations in 1967, incorporates the provisions of the 1951 Refugee Convention and abolishes the restriction that flight must be based on events that took place before January 1951.

HISTORICAL OVERVIEW OF THE
U.S. ASYLUM SITUATION

The United States, a country founded by immigrants and refugees, has traditionally pursued a generous policy toward certain groups fleeing persecution.* Since 1975, when the war in Vietnam caused a massive flow of refugees, the country, acting in accordance with its humanitarian values, has accepted about a million refugees from Southeast Asia. This group of asylum seekers is processed and admitted outside the United States in limited numbers and from specially designated countries. At the same time, however, the U.S. Administration has been reluctant to provide protection to asylum seekers who have arrived in the United States in increasing numbers from Central American and Caribbean countries. This latter group of so-called "spontaneous" asylum-seekers come to the United States on their own. Their numbers cannot be limited, and their countries of origin cannot be predetermined.

Cubans in the 1960s and Haitians in the 1970s were the only national groups of any size who considered the United States a country of first asylum. At the beginning of the 1980s, however, the situation changed. A massive American-Cuban boat lift, the "freedom flotilla," brought about 125,000 Cubans to the United States from the port of Mariel in 1980. Starting at about the same time, civil strife and government violence drove hundreds of thousands of Salvadorans out of their country, and a considerable number of them sought refuge in the United States. Haitians, who had been arriving in boats and often applying for political asylum since 1971, continued to arrive in significant numbers due to the political and economic conditions in their home country. Smaller numbers of Nicaraguans, opposing the Sandinista government, and Guatemalans, fleeing a counterinsurgency campaign that reached its high point in 1982, also came to seek protection in the United States after 1980. Besides

---

*   There were, of course, noteworthy exceptions. See, for example, Daniel S. Wyman, The Abandonment of the Jews: America and the Holocaust 1941-1945, Pantheon Books, 1984, 444pp.

Latin Americans, thousands of Iranians came to the United States to seek asylum in 1979. Finally, starting in 1982, several thousand Afghans, unwilling to wait in refugee camps in Pakistan for refugee selection, came directly to the United States seeking asylum.

These groups have encountered and continue to face a number of alarming practices that are designed by the immigration authorities and the government to deter them from coming to the United States or from applying for asylum. These practices include long-term detention of asylum seekers of all national origins; stopping Haitians on the high seas and returning them to their country; and arresting thousands of Central Americans, mainly Salvadorans and Guatemalans, and forcing them to return to their countries. All of the above violate both national and international legal and humanitarian obligations and threaten to erode the entire legal system that has been developed, both internationally and nationally, in order to protect these especially vulnerable people.

The history of the United States asylum and refugee law until 1980 was largely determined by reactions to specific emergency situations. By favoring people fleeing from governments and social systems that were considered hostile to the United States, U.S. policies reflected geographical and ideological biases. During that period, the Attorney General used three procedures within the general immigration framework to permit aliens to enter or remain in the country. There were no specific provisions providing for asylum.

The Attorney General could a) grant *withholding of deportation* at his discretion to aliens demonstrating a "clear probability of persecution"; b) grant *conditional entry status* to a limited number of refugees from overseas fleeing a communist or Middle Eastern country because of persecution based on race, religion, or political opinion; or c) *parole* an unlimited number of refugees temporarily into the country from overseas "for emergency reasons or for reasons deemed strictly in the public interest" without ideological and geographic limitations.

In 1968, the United States signed and ratified the *1967 United Nations (U.N.) Protocol Relating to the Status of Refugees*. This international instrument bound the country to apply the provisions of the *1951 U.N. Convention Relating to the Status of Refugees* without discrimination against race, religion or country of origin. The Convention defines those persons who are considered to be refugees.* It also obliges the contracting states to comply with the principle of "non-refoulement," which is to refrain from forcibly returning refugees to situations in their countries of origin which threaten their life or freedom.** Some U.S. legal experts contended that national regulations in effect at that point provided sufficient flexibility to permit compliance with the new international standard, and thus, that national legal changes were unnecessary. In practice, however, the immigration authorities were not willing to take advantage of the flexibility of the existing regulations. They continued to stick to restrictive and discriminatory criteria and did not adhere to the Protocol. Courts reviewing withholding of deportation or exclusion cases applied the new standard inconsistently.

This lack of compliance with the new international standard after 1968 aroused Congressional concern. Members of Congress sought to ensure compliance with the U.N. Protocol which finally led to the passage of the *Refugee Act of 1980*. This new act adopted the international refugee definition, as incorporated in the U.N. Protocol, for the determination of asylum claims both abroad and within the United States. It established an asylum procedure for aliens in the United States and a procedure for refugee admissions from overseas. Also, it provided a standard for uniform and non-ideological refugee eligibility. It further eliminated conditional entry and the discretionary power of the Attorney General to parole large groups of people into the country. The principle of "non-refoulement" was also incorporated into U.S. law by amending the withholding of deportation provision*** and by removing the Attorney General's discretion in granting this relief. Congress passed this law in order to institutionalize these international principles in domestic law and to force the immigration authorities to act without ideological and geographical biases.

---

*   Article 1, paragraph 2, of the Convention Relating to the Status of Refugees of 1951.

**   Article 33 of the Convention Relating to the Status of Refugees.

***   Section 243(h) of the Immigration and Nationality Act (INA).

U.S. ASYLUM: PROCEDURES AND CRITERIA

General

The Law

The United States is bound both by national law and international treaties to provide special treatment and protection to asylum seekers. National and international law provide standards and procedures to determine which aliens meet the criteria for refugee protection. The Immigration and Nationality Act (INA) of 1952, as amended by the Refugee Act of 1980, along with a number of regulations of the Immigration and Naturalization Service (INS) and the Administrative Procedure Act, provide the domestic legal basis for these procedures. The 1967 U.N. Protocol relating to the Status of Refugees, to which the United States acceded in 1968, provides the international legal basis.

The Authorities Involved

Decision making bodies are: the district directors of the Immigration and Naturalization Service (INS), which is an agency of the Justice Department; immigration judges and the Board of Immigration Appeals (BIA), which are administrative bodies within the Department of Justice, but separate from the INS; and ultimately, federal district courts, federal circuit courts, and the U.S. Supreme Court. The Bureau of Human Rights and Humanitarian Affairs (BHRHA) of the State Department has an advisory function within the process. Nongovernmental organizations that are also involved include lawyers' organizations, human rights organizations, religious organizations and the representative of the United Nations High Commissioner for Refugees.

The Steps of the Procedure

The 1980 Refugee Act basically provides for two types of procedures for the determination of refugee status according to the U.N. Protocol. One is the *asylum procedure* provided for aliens who are physically in, or seek to enter the United States. Aliens admitted this way are called "asylees." The other procedure is the *overseas refugee admission process*. Aliens admitted under this procedure are called "refugees." They apply and are processed outside the United States in overseas countries at especially designated locations. Both groups of applicants, in the United States and abroad, have to substantiate a personal history of either past persecution or a well-founded fear of future persecution. These criteria are examined on a case-by-case basis. Both refugee and asylee status are granted at the discretion of the government. The only obligation of the U.S. government is not to deport refugees to a country in which they face situations which threaten their life or freedom (principle of non-refoulement). This obligation is fulfilled through the mechanism of withholding of deportation or exclusion.*

Methods of Obtaining Political Asylum in the U.S.

A person seeking admission to, or who is in the United States, may undertake *affirmative action* in order to be granted asylum by applying in the first instance to an INS district director. If the alien has been placed under deportation or exclusion proceedings, he/she may undertake *defensive action* by applying to the immigration judge in charge of the proceedings. In the latter case the asylum claim is treated additionally as a request for withholding of deportation or exclusion.** The Refugee Act grants the right to apply for asylum to aliens claiming a well-founded fear of persecution in their home countries

---

*   Section 243(h) of the Immigration and Nationality Act (INA).

**   Section 208.3(b) of the rules issued pursuant to the INA.

regardless of whether they have made a legal entry into the United States.* Thus an alien is entitled to apply for asylum whether or not he/she has travel documents, or has been found "excludable" or "deportable."**

Applying With an INS District Director

After having filed an asylum application with the district director, the applicant is interviewed under oath by a special INS examiner in a nonadversarial manner. The applicant has the right to be represented by his/her own counsel. He/she has to be informed about this right and of the availability of free legal services. There is, however, no right to appointed counsel for an alien who does not have the financial means to pay for a lawyer. Counsel may appear and participate in the interview. The interview is supposed to provide the district director with any information not contained in the asylum application and with a basis for assessing the applicant's credibility. The applicant has the right to a full and fair hearing. He/she may call and examine witnesses and present whatever evidence is available to support his/her claim.

According to regulations, the district director must seek an opinion from the Bureau for Human Rights and Humanitarian Affairs (BHRHA) of the Department of State on each asylum application. The district director forwards the application to the BHRHA including his own assessment of whether or not the case has merit. State Department officials do not ordinarily explain their advisory opinions. The applicant may inspect, explain and rebut an opinion that is made part of the record. After the district director has received the BHRHA's opinion, a decision is issued in writing which should explain the

---

* Section 208(a) of the rules issued pursuant to the INA.

** Those aliens who do not have valid travel documents and are apprehended at the border are subject to exclusion; those without documentation apprehended within the country are subject to deportation. In the former case, the alien has to establish why he/she should be admitted to the U.S. In the latter, the burden of proof is on the U.S. government to show why the alien is to be deported.

reasons underlying it.*

Asylum may be granted by the Attorney General to "any person who is outside of his/her country of nationality and who is unable or unwilling to return to, and is unable or unwilling to avail him/herself of the protection of that country *because of persecution or a well-founded fear of persecution* on account of race, religion, nationality, membership in a particular social group, or political opinion."**

The application has to be denied if the applicant is not a refugee according to the definition, if he/she has been firmly resettled in another country, if he/she has committed a serious crime, presents a security risk to the U.S., or is found to have persecuted another individual. Even if the applicant is able to meet the requisite criteria and no mandatory grounds for denial of asylum are involved, he/she is not entitled to be granted asylum. The decision to grant asylum is at the discretion of the district director. Discretionary grounds for denial of asylum are an outstanding offer of resettlement by a third nation, if this would be in the public interest, applicant's fraud and circumvention of U.S. immigration laws.***

According to a study by the General Accounting Office (GAO),**** the decisions frequently contain little or no elaboration of the applicant's circumstances as these relate to the law or preceding decisions; nor is there explanation why an applicant had been approved or refused. The district director's decision cannot be appealed. The only way to get the case reexamined at this instance is by means of a motion to reconsider the decision and seek a

---

*   Section 208.8(b) of the rules issued pursuant to the INA.

**   Section 208(a) and 101(a)(42)(A) of the INA.

***   Section 208.8(f)(2) of the rules issued pursuant to the INA.

****   The General Accounting Office is the U.S. Congress' research body. In this study, it examined the asylum practices and procedures at the INS and State Department by trying to determine whether asylum applications were being fairly treated regardless of the applicants' countries of origin, with a particular focus on Central American refugees. The review covered 1,450 asylum applications and INS files of applicants from El Salvador, Poland, Nicaragua and Iran from 1984. The study was released in January 1987.

new advisory opinion upon the submission of "significant" evidence not considered previously.

Applying With an Immigration Judge

After an asylum application has been denied by a district director, the alien is placed under deportation or exclusion proceedings with an immigration judge. At this point, he/she may renew his/her asylum application. If the alien has not yet applied with a district director, he/she is able to apply for asylum with an immigration judge or any further appeals body. There is no limit for the submission of an asylum request; claims may be asserted at any time the alien is physically present in the U.S.

By regulation, applications for asylum at this level "shall also be considered as requests for withholding of deportation or exclusion pursuant to Sec. 243(h)." This remedy is mandated if the alien is able to establish that "his/her life or freedom would be threatened" upon return on account of race, religion, nationality, membership in a particular social group, or political opinion.* It is a temporary and country-specific remedy. Grounds for ineligibility for withholding of deportation or exclusion are participation in the persecution of others, conviction of a particularly serious crime and being considered a danger to the security of the United States.**

The procedure with an immigration judge is similar to that followed under the jurisdiction of a district director except for its adversarial character. In immigration proceedings the authorities are represented by a trial attorney.

Appealing Decisions of Immigration Judges

The decision of an immigration judge may be appealed by either party to the Board of Immigration Appeals (BIA), an administrative appeals tribunal. It is separate from the INS, but within the Department of Justice, appointed by and under the supervision of the Attorney General. The powers of the Board

---

*   Sec. 243(h)(1) of the INA.

**   Sec. 243(h)(2) of the INA.

are broad and plenary. The Board is in no way bound by the immigration judge's determination. Ordinarily, the BIA bases its determination of the case on a review of the file and does not hear the applicant's testimony. The review is therefore limited to the matters developed on the record below. It will remand matters for appropriate proceedings in the immigration court.

The decision of the BIA may be appealed to either a federal district court -- if the alien has been ordered excluded -- or a U.S. circuit court -- if the alien has been ordered deported -- and further to the U.S. Supreme Court. Courts may review errors of law, including violations of statutes or the Constitution, as well as the factual basis and administrative discretion. Generally, however, the level of judicial review is restricted to the administrative record of the proceeding below.

Since the beginning of 1983, immigration judges and the Board of Immigration Appeals have formed a unit separate from the INS, in response to criticism about the apparent lack of independence of the review and appeals agencies from the organizations rendering the initial decisions.* This unit is called "Executive Office for Immigration Review" (EOIR). Most immigration judges come to immigration courts after having been trial attorneys for the INS. Nonetheless, the EOIR (immigration judges and Board of Immigration Appeals) is said by some to be more sensitive in dealing with asylum issues than the restrictive INS.

Because of the difficulties, the vast majority of applicants never take their claim past the first negative decision. Very few asylum applicants pursue their claims beyond the BIA. According to the study of the General Accounting Office, about 77 percent of the asylum applications examined were submitted only to an INS district director, while 16 percent were filed with immigration judges. Seven percent were denied by district directors and renewed before an immigration judge. Only about one percent of the judges'

---

*   Along with this organizational change, immigration judges ceased to keep separate records of the asylum cases pending and processed by nationality of the applicant and the resolution of the cases. Since then, their worksheets simply count all immigration tasks without differentiation. Accordingly, there are no statistics available on the asylum cases dealt with by immigration judges.

decisions were appealed to the BIA. As of the time of the study (July 1986), no decision had been appealed to the regular courts. The BIA decision in *Matter of Pula*, which liberalized the standard for granting asylum as a matter of discretion, has significantly improved the chances for success in the administrative appeals process and through that the effectiveness of the appeals process as such.*

The Criteria for Decisions on Asylum and Withholding of Deportation

To be eligible for (mandatory) withholding of deportation, an alien must show a clear probability of persecution in the country designated for deportation, on account of race, religion, nationality, membership in a particular social group, or political opinion. The alien must demonstrate that it is more likely than not that he/she would be subject to persecution for one of the grounds specified.**

To be eligible for asylum, an alien must meet the refugee definition according to the U.N. Protocol, which has been incorporated by the Refugee Act. This definition requires him/her to show persecution or a well-founded fear of persecution in a particular country on account of race, religion, nationality, membership in a particular social group, or political opinion.

It is generally agreed that an applicant must show more than a subjective fear of persecution, ordinarily through objective evidence that supports the applicant's claims. Threats to life or freedom, such as prolonged detention without charge or trial, significant restriction on freedom of movement, denial of civil and political rights, torture, and disappearances by a government constitute acts of persecution. Persecution may also relate to private individuals or groups, such as "death squads" or "vigilante" groups, if the government actually

---

* Matter of Pula, Interim Decision 3033 (BIA 1987); see details about the decision in the section on "Discretionary Denial of Asylum."

** U.S. Supreme Court in INS v. Stevic, 467 U.S. 407 (1984).

endorses persecution by them or is unable or unwilling to protect citizens against their actions.

The burden of proof required to establish eligibility for asylum is lower than that required for withholding of deportation. In a landmark decision in March 1987,* the U.S. Supreme Court held that the INS was wrong in applying the more restrictive "clear probability of persecution" standard in asylum cases, when it should be limited to cases involving withholding of deportation. The Court argued that a refugee's claims of fear, supported by objective evidence demonstrating that a reasonable person under the same circumstances would fear persecution, is sufficient to prove a well-founded fear of persecution. In effect, the decision liberalized the eligibility standard for asylum by diminishing the level of concrete evidence needed for the establishment of an asylum claim.

Another important aspect of this decision is that the Supreme Court based its interpretation of the refugee definition, in part, on the UNHCR guidelines of the Handbook on Procedures and Criteria for Determining Refugee Status. The UNHCR guidelines stress that the UN refugee definition attaches much importance to the subjective element of fear which makes an assessment of the asylum applicant's credibility indispensable where the case is not sufficiently clear from the facts on the record. While the element of fear is a state of mind and a subjective condition, the qualification of this fear as well-founded refers to the objective situation. Both elements have to be taken into consideration. While the INS continues, essentially, to ignore the UNHCR guidelines, other courts and administrative tribunals have started to utilize them.

The INS generally does not follow the Supreme Court's decision in *INS v. Cardoza-Fonseca*. According to the INS regulations, "the applicant must have actually been persecuted, or (be able to) show good reason why he/she fears persecution." The applicant must seek to demonstrate that his/her fear is well-founded by evidence that is both objective and particular to him/her.

In the wake of *Cardoza-Fonseca*, the Board of Immigration Appeals

---

*   U.S. Supreme Court in INS v. Cardoza-Fonseca, 107 S.Ct.1207 (March 1987).

(BIA) changed its standard of proof of a well-founded fear of persecution. The applicant now has to show, instead of the former clear probability of persecution standard, "that a reasonable person in his/her circumstances would fear persecution ... even where its likelihood is significantly less than clearly probable."* The BIA held that, beyond that different standard of fear, much of the overruled decision remained intact. In particular, the four elements that an alien must demonstrate in order to establish a well-founded fear of persecution were still valid: 1) the alien possesses a belief or characteristic that a persecutor seeks to overcome by punishment of some sort; 2) the persecutor is aware, or could become aware, that the alien possesses the characteristic that is the basis for persecution; 3) the persecutor has the capability to carry out persecution; and 4) the persecutor has the inclination to punish the alien.**

While liberalizing the standard of proof to be met by applicants in order to demonstrate that a fear of persecution is "well-founded," the Supreme Court failed to define the term "persecution" more precisely thus leaving a door to adjudicating authorities to narrow its interpretation.

On the basis of the Supreme Court decision in *Cardoza-Fonseca*, asylum applicants, whose applications were denied because the more stringent "clear probability" standard had been applied, were able to reopen their cases. In this context, it is significant to note that the Attorney General announced that Nicaraguans in the United States with a well-founded fear of persecution would not be deported, and encouraged those whose claims had been denied to reapply. He directed the INS to expedite and re-evaluate Nicaraguan asylum applications in light of the Supreme Court decision. The application of this decision *only* to Nicaraguan asylum cases demonstrates the Administration's failure to implement favorable asylum decisions in an unbiased and non-discriminatory way to asylum seekers of whatever nationality.

---

*   Matter of Mogharrabi, Interim Dec. 3028 (BIA 1987).

**   Matter of Acosta, Interim Dec. 2986 (BIA March 1, 1985).

Significance of Civil War or Severe
Disturbances of Public Order

Internal or military strife in an applicant's home country is not, in itself, sufficient justification for the granting of asylum. The alien must demonstrate that he/she may experience persecution under one or more of the five categories in the Refugee Act. The BIA has noted that aliens fearing personal reprisals or fleeing general conditions of violence and upheaval in their countries do not qualify for asylum for those reasons despite a well-founded fear of persecution. This means that it is not enough for the applicant to base a claim for asylum on general problems in a country that endanger all citizens; it is necessary to give specific reasons and evidence why he/she is likely to be targeted.

The BIA has interpreted this requirement in situations of widescale civil strife or general repression, such as in El Salvador and Haiti, in a very disturbing way that can lead to illogical and unjust results. The Board has stated, for instance, that the threat against the life of a Salvadoran applicant was insufficient because it was representative of the general level of violence in El Salvador.*

> A 27-year old native and citizen of El Salvador left her country "because of threats that she had received by the guerrillas that, if she did not leave her job as a kindergarten teacher in a government school, something bad would happen." She testified that these threats were received by the school personnel and, in addition, by herself in the form of written messages under the door of her home.**

The immigration judge denied the applicant's claim for political asylum stating among other things that:

> these threats were general in nature ... and part of the pattern of guerrilla warfare in the ongoing civil war occurring in El Salvador since 1978 or 1979.

---

*   Matter of Chicas, Int. Dec. 2970 (BIA 1984).

** File provided by CARECEN (Central American Refugee Center), Hempstead, Long Island.

This means, in effect, that the higher the general level of violence, terror and persecution in a country, the more burden there is upon the applicant to show individual targeting. A federal court of appeals called this approach a "clear error of law" and went on to state that:

> ... the significance of a specific threat to an individual's life or freedom is not lessened by the fact that the individual resides in a country where the lives and freedom of a large number of persons are threatened. If anything, ... that fact may make the threat more serious and credible.*

According to immigration law experts, the BIA has started to base denials of asylum claims, especially in the context of civil war and civil strife, on a narrowing interpretation of political opinion and persecution. The Board also tends to focus on individual actions and motivations while neglecting the political context in which they occur.**

In *Desir v. INS,* a Haitian asylum applicant based his claim on beatings, imprisonment, and assault by Ton Ton Macoutes who wanted to extort property from him. The BIA denied the claim by characterizing these actions as a personal conflict. The Ninth Circuit Court of Appeals overruled the BIA saying:

> The Haitian government under Duvalier operated as a kleptocracy, or government by thievery, ... The Ton Ton Macoutes ... formed the heart of the system ... Because the Macoutes are an organization created for political purposes, they bring politics to the villages of Haiti. To challenge the extortion by which the Macoutes exist, is to challenge the underpinnings of the political system.***

The INS and BIA have denied applications from persons who claim to be potential victims of both parties for choosing to remain neutral in an ongoing struggle.

A native and citizen of El Salvador had been a member of the

---

*   Bolanos-Hernandez v. INS, 749 F. 2d 1316, 1323 (9th Cir. 1984).

** Refugee Reports, November 11, 1988, "Board of Immigration Appeals Takes Narrow View of 'Persecution' in Context of Civil War."

*** Quoted in "Board of Immigration Appeals Takes Narrow View ..." op.cit.

right-wing Partido Nacional de Reconciliación, the army and a voluntary civilian police squad guarding against guerrilla infiltration for the government. When he refused to join the guerrillas, who considered him to be particularly useful because of his former membership in these groups, they threatened to kill him unless he joined them or left the country. Since the guerrillas had killed five of his friends and had used similar tactics to recruit his brother -- whom he believes they may have subsequently killed -- he took the threat seriously and left the country in order to apply for political asylum in the United States.*

While the Department of State conceded that the applicant had indicated his commitment and "desire to remain neutral and not be affiliated with any political group," the immigration judge determined that any danger he might be subject to was not because of his political opinion. Subsequently, the BIA held that neutrality did not constitute a political opinion.

In a very important decision, however, the United States Court of Appeals for the Ninth Circuit overruled these decisions by recognizing that neutrality in the face of forced recruitment from either side in a civil war situation like that in El Salvador constitutes a political opinion for which a reasonable person could have a well-founded fear of persecution.**

In 1988, in another significant decision, the United States Court of Appeals for the Fourth Circuit applied a liberal persecution standard in *M.A. v. INS* by holding that the Salvadoran applicant who had refused to participate in the actions of the Salvadoran armed forces was likely to be punished for this refusal. The court did not require the applicant to produce evidence that he had been individually threatened by the authorities, but objective evidence that members of his group (those with the same political beliefs) are routinely subject to persecution. The court stated:

> Where the military engages in internationally condemned acts of violence with which the asylum seeker sincerely does not

---

*   Bolanos-Hernandez v. INS, supra.

** Ibid.

wish to be associated, in light of the UNHCR, the only relevant factor is the likelihood that the alien will be punished.

Alternative Refuge Within the Country of Persecution

The BIA has suggested that the applicant must show that the threat of persecution exists for him/her country-wide.* The Board has denied asylum because the applicant has failed to try to escape persecution in a particular place by moving to another place.

The founder of a taxi cooperative in San Salvador, capital of El Salvador, based his claim for political asylum on the assertion that he was attacked by guerrillas for operating his taxi there. The BIA stated:

> In the respondent's case, the facts show that taxi drivers in the city of San Salvador were threatened with persecution by the leftist guerrillas. However, the facts do not show that this threat existed in other cities in El Salvador. It may be the respondent could have avoided persecution by moving to another city in that country. In any event, the respondent's facts did not demonstrate that the guerrillas' persecution of taxi drivers occurred thoughout the country of El Salvador.**

By requiring an applicant to demonstrate that he/she would be persecuted everywhere in the country the BIA imposes an unacceptable burden of proof on him/her.

Level of Evidence

The burden of proof for asylum eligibility is basically on the applicant. He/she must furnish all relevant facts. According to the UNHCR Handbook, the duty to ascertain and evaluate the relevant facts is shared between the applicant and the examiner. It is the UNHCR's experience that cases in which an applicant can provide evidence for all of his/her statements are the exception

---

*   Matter of Acosta, Interim Dec. 2986 (BIA March 1, 1985).

**   Ibid.

rather than the rule. It is, therefore, suggested that "it is frequently necessary to give the applicant the benefit of the doubt."*

No uniform standards have been established for the type and amount of evidence needed to prove a well-founded fear. Federal courts have disagreed on the standard of proof needed. Courts in the Seventh and Ninth Circuit have held that an applicant's testimony alone may suffice if it is credible, persuasive and specific. The BIA itself has acknowledged that an applicant fleeing persecution may have difficulty gaining access to documentary evidence corroborating his/her claim. It has also ruled that an alien's own testimony may suffice if it is the only evidence available and:

> ...the testimony is believable, consistent and sufficiently detailed to provide a plausible and coherent account of the basis of fear.

In some cases, the U.S. Embassy in the country is consulted and asked to verify an alleged incident or event.

Discretionary Denial of Asylum

Finding that a person has a well-founded fear of persecution does not, by itself, entitle that person to be granted asylum. The decision on granting asylum to a person who has established a well-founded fear of persecution is left to the Attorney General's discretion. The scope of INS authority to deny political asylum, once an applicant has proved a well-founded fear, has not been absolutely determined. In making this discretionary decision, district directors, immigration judges and the BIA are required to consider and weigh the positive against any negative factors which may exist in a case. Sometimes, asylum has been denied as a matter of discretion because the applicant used fraudulent travel documents to enter the United States or tried to circumvent orderly overseas refugee admission procedures abroad.

> A 26-year old native of Albania and citizen of Yugoslavia was detained, interrogated, and physically abused by police officials for hours or days at a time on numerous occasions. The

---

*   Handbook on Procedures and Criteria for Determining Refugee Status, part two, B. (2).

police insisted that he was involved in political activities of the Albanian minority in Yugoslavia. One of the periods of detention occurred after he had approached Yugoslav authorities to request travel documents to visit his sister in the United States because the police suspected him of planning to go to the United States to participate in anti-Yugoslav demonstrations organized by Albanians there. He decided to leave Yugoslavia and go to the United States.

Since he was afraid to apply again for a visa at the American Embassy because most of the employees were Yugoslav nationals who, he suspected, might be agents for the Yugoslav government, he applied for and received a passport allowing him to travel to Turkey. In June 1986, he tried to enter the United States by use of a false travel document and was placed under exclusion proceedings. Subsequently, he applied for political asylum.

In his decision, the immigration judge stated that the facts established without a doubt that the applicant had been persecuted in the past and faced a clear probability of persecution in the future. Since the judge deemed the applicant's testimony to be credible, he found him to be eligible for withholding of deportation to Yugoslavia and Albania, but ineligible for asylum as a matter of discretion because he had sought admission to the United States by use of a purchased travel document.*

This attitude fails to consider important aspects, such as: a) the language of the Refugee Act itself, which enables aliens, "irrespective of their immigration status," to apply for asylum in the United States; b) the danger for people who are subject to government repression in requesting travel documen-

---

* Matter of Pula, Interim Decision 3033 (BIA, September 22, 1987).

tation from that government; and c) the difficulty in obtaining U.S. visas, especially for poor people.*

This unfavorable situation has been significantly mitigated by a decision of the Board of Immigration Appeals (BIA) in September 1987.** The BIA held that an alien's manner of entry, whether he/she has circumvented U.S. immigration laws or the orderly refugee admission procedures, is only one of the factors that have to be weighed in exercising discretion about whether asylum should be granted or not. According to the decision, the totality of the circumstances of an alien's flight from the country where he/she fears persecution has to be taken into account, such as: whether the alien has passed through any other countries where he/she could have found safe haven; whether orderly refugee procedures were available in any country he/she passed through; whether he/she has relatives legally in the United States or other personal ties to this country that motivated him/her to seek asylum in the United States rather than elsewhere. The BIA further held that, while the use of fraudulent documents to escape the country itself is not a significant adverse factor, entry with a United States passport, which was fraudulently obtained by the alien from the U.S. government, constitutes serious fraud.

The BIA is concerned particularly with situations in which the alien is able to establish a well-founded fear of persecution, but cannot prove the clear probability of persecution required for withholding of deportation. Discretion-

---

* They have to prove that they have funds for their return trip and their U.S. maintenance, convince the consular officer that they will indeed return after the expiration of their visas. Of more than 71,000 Haitians, for instance, who applied for visas to visit the U.S. in 1988, more than 50 percent were rejected, mainly because consular offices suspected they would try to stay in the U.S. (The New York Times, Nov. 27, 1988, "Rise seen in Haitians fleeing illegally to U.S.")

** Matter of Pula, supra.

ary denial of asylum in such a case could easily lead to the alien's deportation to the country where he/she fears persecution. The BIA suggests that "the danger of persecution should generally outweigh all but the most egregious of adverse factors."*

The availability of a country of first asylum or safe haven, to which aliens can be deported, is frequently used by the BIA as an argument against granting asylum. Mexico is considered by the U.S. immigration authorities to be a country of safe haven for Central American asylum seekers. In a study by Joan Friedland and Jesus Rodriguez y Rodriguez at the Mexico-U.S. Law Institute on this issue,** the authors find that Mexico has demonstrated that it will not accept refugees deported from the United States, who have been rejected for U.S. asylum because they passed through Mexico on their way north. With respect to protection of refugees in Mexico, one must be aware that Mexico is not a signatory to the 1951 Refugee Convention or to the 1967 Protocol. Mexican law does not recognize the term "refugee." In order to be granted asylum in Mexico, the applicant has to establish an actual history of past persecution exclusively for political reasons. This requirement is far narrower than the internationally accepted standard which also includes persecution because of a person's race, religion, nationality and membership in a particular social group.

According to the study, due to these narrow requirements asylum is almost never granted in Mexico. Mexican law gives the government wide discretion to expel aliens. Foreigners, including those granted asylum, may be expelled with no legal process. The authors of the study suggest that "the argument that Mexico is an automatic safe haven or resettlement country for refugees who passed through on their way to the U.S. ignores both current policy and the de-

---

*   Ibid.

** "Seeking Safe Ground: The Legal Situation of Central American Refugees in Mexico," Joan Friedland/Jesus Rodriguez y Rodriguez, Mexico-U.S. Law Institute of the University of San Diego Law School and Legal Research Institute of the National Autonomous University of Mexico, 1987.

gree to which that policy would tighten if Mexico's burden were increased."

Status of Asylum Seekers During Proceedings

Asylum applicants have temporary status pending the outcome of their asylum application. They are to be be granted employment authorization if their asylum application is considered non-frivolous.*

Status of Asylum Seekers After a Final Decision

After the application for asylum has been approved, the applicant is granted asylum for one year and is entitled to obtain work authorization. Asylees are entitled to be issued a Refugee Travel Document. After one year, the case is reviewed. If the asylee still meets the criteria, he/she has the right to apply for permanent legal residence status. This status renders him/her eligible for U.S. citizenship, ordinarily after 5 more years.

After an application for asylum has finally been denied, immigration judges usually order that, instead of deportation, the alien be given a period of 30 days for "voluntary departure," which may be extended by the district director. This protects the alien from being barred from entering the United States in the future as a deportee who has violated U.S. immigration laws.**

An asylum applicant who has only been granted withholding of deportation or exclusion is not entitled to become a permanent legal resident and may, moreover, be deported to a third country. According to the GAO study, few applicants who have been denied asylum are deported. This is to a large extent due to practical difficulties in locating aliens in order to carry out deportation. Among the four countries examined, El Salvador, Iran, Nicaragua and

---

*   8 C.F.R. Section 274a.13(a) as recodified by new regulations in 1988 as a result of the Immigration Reform and Control Act. See the section on "Work Authorization."

** Moreover he/she ordinarily will not be subjected to criminal penalties or sanctions for unauthorized entry into the U.S.

Poland, only applicants from El Salvador had been deported. In fiscal year 1988, for instance, the INS deported 3,691 Salvadorans and 200 Nicaraguans.* Although both groups of nationals face political persecution in their homelands, the Administration tended to return Salvadorans while allowing many Nicaraguans to stay.**

At the end of 1988, however, the U.S. government allocated considerable financial and personnel resources in south Texas where most Central Americans enter the United States to enhance deportation activities. The INS has also started to expedite decisions on affirmative asylum applications and to detain rejected applicants in order to ensure their deportation. This policy is pursued indiscriminately affecting all asylum applicants with the exception of Nicaraguans who, for the time being, are detained but not deported.***

In general only persons belonging to groups that have been granted Extended Voluntary Departure (EVD) are temporarily exempted from deportation.****

Recent Legal Developments

In April 1988, the INS published for public comment a revised version of an earlier proposal of asylum regulations. + The earlier proposal from August 1987+ + would have vested INS asylum officers with exclusive jurisdiction over asylum cases and would have ousted immigration judges from asylum and withholding determinations. The proceedings with INS officials would have been non-adversarial, depriving asylum applicants of the opportunity to present

---

*   The New York Times, Sept. 11, 1988, "Salvadoran Issues a Refugee Appeal."

**   On July 8, 1987, the Attorney General announced that Nicaraguans with a well-founded fear of persecution would not be deported. Refugee Reports/August 14, 1987.

***   See the section on "New INS Policy Towards Central American Asylum Seekers."

****   For details on EVD, see the section on "The Need for Temporary Protection."

+   53 Fed. Reg. 11,300-10 (April 6, 1988) in 65 Interpreter Releases 386-96 (April 11, 1988).

+ +   52 Fed. Reg. 32,552-61 (Aug. 28, 1987) in 64 Interpreter Releases 989-91, 1000-09 (1987).

their cases in an open and impartial hearing with an immigration judge. In addition, these officers would have kept on using the State Department's annual "Country Reports on Human Rights Practices" as a principal source of information and would have perpetuated a situation in which foreign policy considerations are decisive in the asylum adjudication process. A virtual storm of protests caused the INS to drop its plans to issue this proposal.

While a number of provisions from the original proposal have been kept in the revised one, there are also some significant changes. Most importantly, immigration judges will continue to exercise their present function, which is to adjudicate asylum and withholding requests. The current rules retain the creation of asylum officers replacing district directors in their function to determine asylee status. These officers will receive special training in international law and relations provided by the INS Assistant Commissioner for Refugees, Asylum and Parole and the Director of the Asylum, Policy and Review Unit of the Justice Department's Office of Legal Policy under the direction of the INS in Washington. By establishing these asylum officers, INS seeks to develop expertise in the field of asylum adjudication and a higher degree of uniformity in decision making. This effort is to be welcomed.

The new rules no longer give preference to Department of State country reports as a source for evaluating the human rights situation in a country, but allow asylum officers to rely also on nongovernmental sources. In a clear departure from former U.S. government policy in determining refugee status, the revised proposal allows asylum applicants to demonstrate that persons in their position, and not only the applicants individually, could be subject to persecution. It requires, however, that the applicant establish 1) that there is a pattern of persecution of groups of persons similarly situated and 2) that his/her own inclusion and identification with that group is such that his/her fear of persecution is reasonable.

The currently proposed rules do not seek any longer to guide asylum adjudicators in their exercise of discretion on whether to deny asylum on the basis of factors such as destruction of immigration documents or attempt to obtain fraudulently status in the U.S. This provision, which had been part of the earlier proposal, had been opposed strongly since it did not take into account that these factors are inherent in the refugee experience. According to the revised proposal, decisions by asylum officers are subject to review by higher officials in the INS central office and by the office of the Deputy Attorney General.

In addition to these first positive steps towards a substantial improvement of the asylum determination process, new problems have been created and chronic problems remain. The current regulations enable immigration judges to limit the examination of evidence that is presented in exclusion or deportation hearings where a mandatory ground for denial of asylum is involved. This is the case if asylum seekers have participated in the persecution of others, have committed a serious crime in the United States, or pose a danger to the security of the United States. In any of these three cases the judge would not need to inquire into the nature of the persecution feared. Such an approach contradicts the discretionary nature of asylum and its particular purpose of protecting especially vulnerable people. Efficient protection requires a balancing of the gravity of the offense against the gravity of the persecution feared in each case. This part of the proposed regulations has encountered most resistance among refugee advocacy groups.

Moreover, motions by an asylum seeker facing deportation to reopen deportation or exclusion proceedings will be denied unless he/she is able to give reasons for the failure to apply for asylum earlier and to introduce evidence that was previously unavailable. Given the humanitarian purpose of the asylum determination procedure, this proposal is unduly restrictive. It fails to give asylum seekers the benefit of the doubt, as set forth by the guidelines in the UNHCR Handbook on Procedures and Criteria for Determining Refugee Status.

One of the basic problems of the present asylum adjudication process is the lack of an independent and impartial arbiter. The INS currently adjudicating asylum claims is in charge of two essentially incompatible tasks: refugee adjudication which should crucially aim at protecting the vital interests of a group of particularly vulnerable people; and immigration policy which is largely based on U.S. domestic and foreign policy interests. The new rules perpetuate this system.

As of the writing of this report, the proposed regulations were not issued yet in their final form, in part due to opposition within the INS.

Methods of Obtaining Refugee Status in the Overseas Admission Process:*

The 1980 Refugee Act provides for refugee admissions from abroad, limited by yearly numerical ceilings. After consulting with the Judiciary Committees of Congress, the President sets an annual plan for refugees to be admitted each fiscal year as "justified by humanitarian concerns or ... the national interest" and specifies their countries (or regions) of origin. The President is also authorized under the Act to respond to an unforeseen, emergency refugee situation and to admit refugees for a period of up to twelve months. The executive's "parole power," which had become the principal mechanism for admitting refugees before the passage of the Refugee Act, is used under the Act only if there are "compelling reasons," such as humanitarian ones in individual cases, as opposed to regular admission.

Once the numbers and allocations are established, the Attorney General has authority to admit persons who meet the refugee criteria of the 1980 Refugee Act. Determinations as to who are refugees within the statutory definition are to be made on a case-by-case basis. Under the INS regulations for the Overseas Refugee Admission Process, the Attorney General may adopt processing priorities based on such goals as reuniting families and on factors such as a refugee's close association with the U.S.

Although the Refugee Act's central purpose was to remove ideological and geographical limitations in the Overseas Process, its implementation, in effect, establishes quotas and favors refugees from particular countries and regions and excludes refugees from others. It tends to be a group determina-

---

*   Section 207 of the Immigration and Nationality Act.

tion process instead of providing for refugee determination on a case-by-case basis, as the 1980 Refugee Act requires.

The admission of Armenians from the Soviet Union reveals the character of the Overseas Refugee Admission Process. The total ceiling for the admission of refugees for 1988 was originally 68,500.* The increased emigration of Armenians and Jews in the spring of 1988, however, caused the President to use his power to respond to an unforeseen emergency situation by increasing the ceiling for Eastern Europe and the Soviet Union by 15,000, thus raising the overall ceiling to 83,500. Twelve thousand of the additional places were allocated for Soviet Armenians, 2,000 for Soviet Jews, and 1,000 for East Europeans. The planned admission of such a large number of Armenians at a time when actual processing of refugees from other regions of the world had already developed a huge backlog stirred up controversy among refugee advocates about whether these admissions had been properly conducted. According to *The New York Times,***U.S. officials asserted that thousands of Armenians from the Soviet Union were admitted to the United States as refugees, although the majority of them did not meet the refugee criteria.

Both the designation of regional ceilings and the actual admissions reflect the Administration's failure to comply with its obligation not to discriminate invidiously in admitting refugees. The overall ceiling for refugees for fiscal year 1989 is 94,000. This figure is less than half the number of refugees admitted in 1981, the year the Reagan Administration took office. On November 9, 1988, the president determined original allocations as follows: 53,000 for South East Asia (25,000 for Vietnamese within an orderly departure program, 28,000 for other South East Asians), 24,500 for Eastern Europe and the Soviet Union (6,500 for Eastern Europe and 18,000 for the Soviet Union), 7,000 for

---

*   38,000 for East Asia, 15,000 for Eastern Europe and the Soviet Union, 9,000 for the Near East and South Asia, 3,500 for Latin America and 3,000 for Africa and an unallocated and unfunded number of 4,000.

** The New York Times, May 29, 1988, and editorial of June 6, 1988.

the Near East/South Asia region, 3,500 for Latin America and 2,000 for Africa. In January 1989, President Reagan raised the Soviet quota by 39 percent to 25,000 by cutting the quota for Vietnamese by 5,500 to 19,500, the quota for other South East Asians by 1,000 to 27,000, and the quota for refugees from the Near East/South Asia -- which includes Afghanistan and Iran -- by 500 to 6,500.*

The overall higher level, 94,000 as compared to 83,500 in 1988, is mainly for the benefit of Soviet citizens, and to some extent for Amerasians and Vietnamese. Other regions had to suffer serious cutbacks: the ceiling for Africa has been reduced from 3,000 in FY 1988 to 2,000 in FY 1989; the ceiling for Near/East South Asia from 9,000 to 7,000. The designation of specific countries as of special humanitarian concern favors refugees from communist or leftist countries: in Africa, mostly refugees from Ethiopia have been designated for admission; in Latin America and the Caribbean, mostly Cuba and Nicaragua have been named countries of special humanitarian concern. Refugees from countries such as Guatemala, El Salvador and Haiti are virtually excluded from being eligible for the refugee admission process.

The overall ceiling for refugees in fiscal year 1988 was 83,500. In 1988, the largest percentage of refugees was admitted from Indochina (particularly Vietnam and Cambodia); the next largest from Eastern Europe and the Soviet Union; a lesser number of Iranians and Afghans; and a few thousand Ethiopians and Nicaraguans. Refugees fleeing other countries were essentially barred from coming to the United States through the overseas process. In its explanation of both the regional ceilings and the country specific allocations for refugees in FY 1988, the State Department cited political repression as the cause of flight from communist nations, but not from non-communist ones.

Among 629 Africans actually admitted to the U.S. in FY 1988, 441 were from Communist Ethiopia. Among 2,993 refugees admitted from all of Latin America, 2,786 were from leftist Nicaragua, and only 6 from Haiti. For the first time, 24 Guatemalans and 110 Salvadorans were admitted under an allocated reserve for unforeseen refugee admission needs. Actual admissions for 1986

---

*   Source: U.S. Department of State.

and 1987 followed similarly selective patterns: while 1,329 Africans were admitted during 1986, 1,268 were from Ethiopia. Among 1,974 Africans actually admitted in 1987, 1,808 were from Ethiopia. In 1987, the regional admission ceilings were adjusted during the year. This reduced the numbers of Latin American and African refugees who could be admitted, and increased the allowance for Eastern European, Near East and South Asian refugees.*

The INS officials involved in the examination of the cases do not receive special training. Lawyers are not involved in the proceedings. Individuals whose applications have been denied have no right to appeal the decision. In short, the overseas admission procedure lacks any guarantee of due process. It is largely conducted and viewed as an extra-legal process. Furthermore, the INS appears unwilling to act in compliance with recent judicial decisions on asylum in the United States which liberalized the criteria for demonstrating a well-founded fear of persecution. The INS Guidelines for the Overseas Refugee Admission Process, issued in 1983, do not take these new standards into account. The entire system fails to live up to its important mandate to provide large numbers of persons, claiming a well-founded fear of persecution, with a fair and unbiased procedure for the examination of these claims.**

The application for refugee status has to be forwarded to the overseas officer responsible for the area where the applicant is located. This has to be a place outside the United States and generally also outside of the persecuting country,*** or if impossible to do so, at a designated consular office. INS of-

---

* The African ceiling had been revised from 3,500 to 2,000, the Latin American/Caribbean one from 4,000 to 1,000, the Eastern European and Soviet ceiling from 10,000 to 12,300, and the Near East/South Asian one from 8,000 to 10,200.

** For detailed information on the admission of Indochinese refugees see: Refuge Denied: Problems in the Protection of Vietnamese and Cambodians in Thailand and the Admission of Indochinese Refugees into the U.S., Lawyers Committee for Human Rights, 1989.

*** The Refugee Act allows the President, "in special circumstances after appropriate consultation," to specify that certain groups still within the country may be accorded refugee status (e.g., an orderly departure program).

fices are located abroad in Athens (Greece), Bangkok (Thailand), Frankfurt (FRG), Mexico City and Guadalajara (Mexico), Hong Kong, Manila (Philippines), Montevideo (Uruguay), Rome (Italy), Seoul (South Korea), Singapore and Vienna (Austria). There are waiting lists maintained for each refugee group designated by presidential determination.

An applicant for refugee status is interviewed by an INS officer. He/she is not represented by counsel. The application is approved if the alien meets the refugee definition set up by the 1980 Refugee Act, is not firmly resettled in any foreign country, is determined to be of special humanitarian concern and is admissible as an immigrant under the Act.* Moreover he/she must not have participated in the persecution of others on account of race, religion, nationality, political opinion or membership in a particular social group. Most grounds of inadmissibility as an immigrant are either automatically waived for refugees** or may be waived at the Attorney General's discretion. In addition, each applicant must submit to a medical examination and have a sponsor, a person or organization that guarantees his/her transportation to the United States.

If refugee status is denied by the hearing officer, INS Guidelines*** provide that the decision be reviewed by a supervisory official and the officer-in-charge. The applicant is not informed of the basis for denying the application. There is no transcript of the interview. The file is confidential and accessible only to U.S. government officials. There is no formal appeal process and no judicial review.

After an approving decision has been rendered by an INS official abroad, the refugee will be admitted conditionally by the district director at the port of entry in the U.S., provided that he/she arrives within four months of the date of approval. After one year of physical presence in the U.S., the refugee is entitled to apply for legal permanent residence. His/her other rights and legal

---

*   Section 207(c)(1) of the INA.

**   Such as lack of labor certification, lack of a valid passport or visa, likelihood that he/she will become a public charge, or illiteracy.

***   "Worldwide Guidelines for Overseas Refugee Processing," issued by the INS in 1983.

status are equivalent or superior to those of asylees.

Processing such large numbers of refugees abroad has caused serious problems which became especially acute in 1988. Refugees who had been approved by INS officials abroad, and were thus ready to depart, were not being processed by the State Department because of financial problems. Authority had been given to move 83,500 refugees with a budget for 68,500. Month by month, the admission of refugees to the United States was following a feast or famine pattern for FY 88, with minimal processing for all regions outside of Eastern Europe/USSR during the first half of the year, and an anticipated glut of refugee processing during the final quarter.* As of March 31, the end of the first half of FY 88, less than one quarter of the refugees authorized per regional ceiling had been admitted, on average, to the United States from all regions other than the USSR/Eastern Europe.

Approximately 75 to 80 percent of all applications for refuge in the United States and 90 to 95 percent of all applications that are actually approved are processed in overseas countries. This demonstrates the importance of the overseas process.

---

* Refugee Reports, June 24, 1988, "End of Year 'Bulge' Predicted on Refugee Admissions."

U.S. ASYLUM: POLICIES AND PRACTICES

Detention

Ghafoor M.* from Afghanistan decided to leave Afghanistan after having been imprisoned by the Afghan government for 18 days and having been tortured with electric shock because of anti-government posters that had been found at the bank where he worked. He was suspected of having a brother fighting with the mujahedeen. After having been forced to join the Afghan Army, he escaped and joined the mujahedeen. Ghafoor, his wife and her sister were able to escape to Pakistan. Since the Secret Police were searching for him, it was not safe for him to stay there either. After inquiries at the U.S. Consulate he learned that he could not come to the U.S. as a refugee because of lack of sponsors. Normal immigration procedures would have taken him at least three years. He managed to come to the U.S. with false travel documents.

Arriving at John F. Kennedy International Airport on September 17, 1984, he, his wife and her sister immediately applied for political asylum in the U.S. Instead of finding the refuge they were hoping to find, they were detained and released on parole only on January 14, 1986; this due to interventions by U.S. human rights groups and Senators.** They were released along with 30 other Afghans who had been detained for up to 18 months because of illegal entry. During the 16 months of their detention, their claims for political asylum were examined, first by an immigration judge and then by the Board of Immigration Appeals (BIA) on appeal. Both the judge and the BIA acknowledged that the applicants had a well-founded fear of persecution and granted withholding

---

*   File provided by the Lawyers Committee for Human Rights, New York City.

** The New York Times, January 10, 1986: "United States to Free 33 Afghans Who Entered Illegally."

of exclusion. They denied, however, the claims to political asylum of the Afghans as a matter of discretion because of their illegal entry into the U.S.

> Ghafoor M.: "It is unfortunate but true that our experiences in Afghanistan and Pakistan and in the first 16 months in the United States have left scars on my wife and me. Especially my wife has suffered greatly from the 16 months imprisonment in the U.S. detention center and still feels physical after-effects. She stays home all day and does not feel well, although we have seen many doctors and she has been taking medicine as well."

The strict policy of detaining undocumented arriving aliens had been abandoned by the U.S. administration in 1954, and a 26-year period followed during which the release policy was liberalized. During this period only a small number of aliens who appeared likely to abscond or to pose a threat to the security of the United States were detained for a significant period. This policy applied to all aliens regardless of whether they had travel documents or were asylum applicants.

In 1982, however, the INS re-established the policy of detaining undocumented aliens arriving at the borders of the United States. This was in response to the influx of over 125,000 Cubans and thousands of Haitians seeking refuge in the United States.* The INS regulations mandate detention of those aliens who arrive without documents or with fraudulent documents and are, therefore, subject to exclusion, and preclude their release.** Parole is possible only for "emergency reasons" (e.g., serious medical condition of the alien) or when it is "strictly in the public interest."*** Those who appear to be inad-

---

* The INS issued the final rule in spite of comments of the UNHCR and 14 other interested parties that it violated the UN Protocol relating to the Status of Refugees, the Refugee Act of 1980 and the Administrative Procedure Act.

** Section 235.3 of the INA.

*** If the alien poses neither a security risk nor a risk of absconding, and is pregnant, juvenile, a beneficiary of an immigrant visa petition filed by a close relative, a witness to a judicial, administrative or legislative proceeding, or if the alien's continued detention is not in the public interest. 8 C.F.R. 212.5(a).

missible on grounds other than lack of travel documents or possession of fraudulent documents are subject to a more liberal release policy. They may be released unless they pose a security risk or are likely to abscond. The regulations put no limit on the duration of detention. It may continue throughout the appeals proceedings.

An alien who has been apprehended within the country and has been placed under deportation proceedings may also be arrested. Once taken into custody by the INS, and pending a deportation hearing, he/she is subject to broad discretion by the Attorney General with regard to his/her release upon his/her own recognizance, or upon the posting of a bond.

As a result of this policy, thousands of aliens, including Afghans, Cubans, Ethiopians, Guatemalans, Haitians, Iranians and Salvadorans, a large number of whom are asylum applicants, have been imprisoned indiscriminately in facilities around the United States with no possibility of release while their cases are adjudicated. At the end of 1988, more than 6,000 aliens were held in these facilities. According to the Lawyers Committee for Human Rights, the largest nationality group in detention, estimated at about 500 persons, is Salvadoran. The average period of detention is six months to one year. Even when release is possible, an alien generally may not be released until he/she finds a sponsor or posts bond. In deportation proceedings, a minimum bond of $500, and usually much more, is required. Indigent refugees may not be able to overcome this obstacle.

By focusing on undocumented aliens, the INS detention program affects asylum seekers heavily. International experience shows that asylum seekers frequently flee persecution in their home countries without travel documents. This fact seems to confirm their emergency situation rather than to give cause for their punishment. The Immigration and Nationality Act (INA) takes this experience into consideration by entitling undocumented as well as documented aliens to apply for asylum. The U.S. Administration, however, penalizes those who are apprehended while trying to enter the country illegally by detaining them and precluding them from release. Those undocumented aliens who manage to enter the country without inspection are curiously favored by the INS policy. Once apprehended within the country and placed under deportation proceedings, the latter group of aliens is subject to a more liberal release policy. This differential treatment of undocumented aliens is without grounds in substance.

The policy of long-term detention is psychologically devastating to many of those who seek asylum in the United States. Confinement occurs under isolated and onerous conditions. The detainees are separated from family and friends and, since the majority of them do not speak English, they are often unable to communicate with the authorities. The physical conditions vary, depending on the facility, but are similar to prison conditions. There are few, if any, social or educational programs available. The frustration detainees suffer during prolonged detention has resulted in suicide attempts and mass hunger strikes.*

In November of 1987, 18 asylum seekers being detained at the INS Service Processing Center at Varick Street in New York City went on a hunger strike that lasted for 29 days.** Most of them had been detained for more than a year. They were protesting the length and conditions of their detention, including incarceration with convicted alien criminals awaiting deportation, overcrowding, lack of recreation and family visits, delayed or denied medical treatment and physical abuse by INS guards. Most of the detainees were released after the hunger strike, some only after several months.

After having been sharply criticized for inhumane conditions, the INS discontinued the use of the Viscount International Hotel at JFK Airport in New York City as a detention facility. Another airport hotel, the Westway, has, however, replaced it, presenting similar problems. While the hunger strikes did not lead to any changes in INS detention policy all released detainees have been replaced by newly arrived asylum seekers discussions on whether to limit the period of detention continue.

Detainees' access to counsel is severely restricted. If they succeed in

---

*   For more details see: Mother of Exiles, Lawyers Committee for Human Rights and Helsinki Watch, 1986.

**   Members Update Newsbrief, Lawyers Committee for Human Rights, Winter 1988.

getting an attorney to represent them, the fact of being detained prevents them from effectively assisting their counsel in preparing the evidence to support their claims. The proceedings, which usually take well over a year, are likely to be even more protracted because of the complex nature of the claims. In many cases, detention results in deterring refugees from exercising their right to apply for asylum or to appeal negative decisions, and in forcing them to return to the countries where they fear persecution. Moreover, this policy of detaining undocumented aliens is designed to deter other aliens from coming to the United States, including those who intend to apply for asylum.

Insofar as the detention policy is designed to deter refugees from applying for asylum or makes them return to territories where their life or freedom is threatened, it violates their statutory right to apply for asylum and the non-refoulement principle set forth by the U.N. Protocol. Moreover, it violates the Refugee Act which requires equal treatment of asylum seekers regardless of their immigration status; the right of asylum seekers not to be deprived of their liberty without due process under the Fifth Amendment of the U.S. Constitution;* and the right not to be penalized or unnecessarily restricted in movement under the 1967 United Nations Protocol.** The detention policy is also inconsistent with international instruments such as the Universal Declaration of Human Rights and the American Convention on Human Rights that both stipulate that nobody shall be subjected to arbitrary arrest or detention, respective-

---

*   Administrative detention of aliens has been approved only as a means of effecting exclusion or deportation, or to protect society from aliens found to be security risks.

**   Article 31 of the U.N. Convention Relating to the Status of Refugees, as incorporated in the UN Protocol, provides that "contracting states shall not apply to such [unlawfully in the country] refugees restrictions other than those which are necessary and such restrictions shall only be applied until their status in the country is regularized..."

In 1981, the Executive Committee of the UNCHR adopted a series of recommendations regarding the protection of asylum seekers in large scale influx. Among numerous other things, it recommended that asylum seekers should not be subject to punishment for illegal entry or restriction of their movement.

ly imprisonment.* Moreover, it contradicts a conclusion of the Executive Committee of the UNHCR of 1986, which includes the United States, stating that detention of refugees should not be automatic.

The detention facilities are owned and operated or leased by the INS. At present, there are eight immigration detention centers. They are located in Miami, Florida; Port Isabel and El Paso, Texas; El Centro, California; Oakdale, Louisiana; New York City; Florence, Arizona; Boston, Massachusetts. In addition, the INS has held aliens in more than 1,000 non-Service contract facilities. The Oakdale facility has a holding capacity for 1,000 aliens and contingency space for up to 5,000 additional detainees in a tent city behind the facility. Some of these facilities are located in urban areas, others in remote areas where it is difficult to find adequate legal representation or social support. Oakdale, Louisiana, for example, the largest detention facility, is located approximately 200 miles from either Houston or New Orleans.

Interdiction of Haitians

Between 1971 and 1981, approximately 35,000 to 45,000 Haitian boat people made their way to the United States. Through 1977, most of these Haitians were detained with bonds set at a minimum of $500, and those released on bond were denied work authorization. Only for a brief period thereafter, the INS agreed to release Haitian boat people without bond and to grant work authorization to them. Beginning in May 1981, a few months after the Reagan Administration took office, all Haitians arriving by boat in Southern Florida without entry documents were detained at Camp Krome outside of Miami, at Fort Allen in Puerto Rico and at federal prisons and detention centers around the United States. On September 29, 1981:

> having found that the entry of undocumented aliens, arriving at the borders of the United States from the high seas, is detrimental to the interests of the U.S.

---

*   Universal Declaration of Human Rights, Art. 9; American Convention on Human Rights, Art. 7,3.

the President proclaimed that:
> The entry of undocumented aliens from the High Seas is hereby suspended and shall be prevented by the interdiction of certain vessels carrying such aliens.*

The program is based on an agreement with the Haitian government,** according to which the U.S. Coast Guard may board vessels bound for the United States and make inquiries about the legal status of the aliens on board. In case of a violation of U.S. law or an appropriate Haitian law, the vessel and the persons aboard may be returned to Haiti. The U.S. agreed to the presence of a representative of the Haitian Navy aboard any U.S. vessel engaged in the Interdiction Program. The agreement also provides that:
> the U.S., having regard for its international obligations pertaining to refugees, does not intend to return to Haiti any Haitian migrants the U.S. determines qualify for refugee status.

Finally, the Haitian Government agreed that all Haitians returned to the country who are not traffickers in illegal migration will not be subject to prosecution for illegal departure.

The entire procedure is highly objectionable from a human rights and a humanitarian point of view. The Administration's Interdiction Program fails to give appropriate weight to the extremely unstable and continuing repressive political situation in Haiti. It is more than unlikely that Haitians under the circumstances of the program would be willing and able to talk about fears of persecution in Haiti. The operation does not protect those among the migrants who

---

* Proclamation No. 4865, 46 Fed.Reg. 48, 107 (1981).

** Interdiction Agreement, Sept. 23, 1981, United States-Haiti, T.I.A.S. No.10,241.

may have a well-founded fear of persecution. The Administration's reference to the protection of refugees in the Interdiction Agreement can only be considered an empty promise.

As of May 10, 1989, 20,421 Haitians have been interdicted and returned to Haiti since the inception of the program.* 3,541 of these were returned in 1987 and 4,564 in 1988 alone,** which represents a dramatic increase over previous years and illustrates clearly the failure of the program to deter Haitians from fleeing their country and attempting to enter the United States. Since the inception of the program, only five Haitians have been allowed to enter the U.S. in order to apply for political asylum. Fewer than 150 persons have been allowed to enter the U.S. because of serious health problems.***

In FY 1985, the year immediately before the fall of the Duvalier dictatorship, 3,971 Haitians were interdicted on the seas. In FYs 1986 and part of 1987, after the fall of the dictatorship, as Haitians were looking forward to their first free elections, interdictions annually declined to 3,247 and 2,807. They rose dramatically after the elections were halted by a massacre.

At the end of January 1989 and on March 24, 1989, the U.S. Coast Guard returned two boats carrying 137 and 101 Haitians respectively. Both groups were interdicted in U.S. waters close to Miami in violation of both the Interdiction Agreement, which calls for interdiction on the high seas, and the non-refoulement principle. The incident revealed numerous irregularities in the conduct of U.S. authorities, including physical abuse of Haitians who resisted being returned to Haiti.****

---

* National Coalition for Haitian Refugees, New York City, based on an INS report on <u>Haitian Migrant Interdiction Operations</u> (HMIO) issued in January 1989, Coast Guard information, news reports and personal observations.

** U.S. Coast Guard, <u>General Law Enforcement Digest of Interdiction Statistics</u>, and <u>Le Nouvelliste</u>, January 12, 1989, "Un nombre record d'Haitiens interceptés en 1988 par les garde-côtes des USA" (record number of Haitians interdicted by the U.S. Coast Guard in 1988).

*** National Coalition for Haitian Refugees, New York City.

**** National Coalition for Haitian Refugees, New York City.

In an especially dramatic incident on March 25, 1989, 250 Haitians packed on a rickety 50-feet sailboat refused to turn themselves in to the approaching Coast Guard vessel at some 150 miles off the shore of Miami. In an unprecedented act of despair, several Haitians threatened to plunge into the ocean and even to throw their babies into the ocean. A woman who actually carried out her threat could only be saved with great difficulty. Only after a 30-hour long pursuit of the Haitian boat were five Coast Guard vessels able to stop it. A Coast Guard officer expressed his concern about the incident saying:

> Haitian people are always putting up a certain resistance to our efforts to stop them, but I have never experienced anything comparable before. The Haitians are a peaceful people. This change of their behavior demonstrates that they have reached a point of enormous frustration.*

Except for five, none of the 20,421 Haitians interdicted since the inception of the program was deemed to have sufficient basis to have his/her asylum claim examined under the administrative process provided for by the Refugee Act. Under the Interdiction Program, the fate of thousands of Haitians is determined in public interviews, without access to counsel, that last only a few minutes. U.S. immigration authorities consider all Haitian boat people to be mere economic migrants because of their poverty, failing to take into account that political repression has caused this situation to a large extent and continues to prevent fundamental changes. It is significant to note that even a Coast Guard report conceded that, besides economic reasons, the "political situation has some bearing" in migrants' decision to leave their country.**

The Interdiction Operation is being carried out in the Windward Passage between Haiti and Cuba, 550 miles away from Miami, Florida, and to a minor extent also off the Miami shore. A Coast Guard cutter carries, in addition to Coast Guard personnel, an INS officer and INS interpreters. During the initial years of the Interdiction Program, the cutter also carried a representative

---

*   Haiti en Marche, 29 March 4 April 1989, "Un Peuple Fuyant L'Holocauste."

** Injustice on the High Seas: U.S. Interdiction of Haitian Boat People, National Coalition for Haitian Refugees, March 1989.

of the Haitian government, but this practice reportedly ceased in the meantime. Once a vessel is sighted by aircraft surveying the area, a group of four to six people, including an INS official and interpreter, boards the vessel. They ask the passengers where they are coming from and heading for and whether they have documents.

On an average, the vessels are packed with 80 to 180 people risking their lives due to the unseaworthiness of the boats and the lack of adequate equipment for such a long trip.* In mass interviews, that usually last one or two minutes per person,** the INS official determines whether the people aboard are afraid of going back to Haiti. The interviews are carried out publicly, without counsel and, during the initial years of the program, in the presence of a Haitian government official, clearly recognizable as such to the Haitian migrants. According to the U.S. government, except for five, none of the Haitians interdicted has presented a bona-fide claim for political asylum.

If the people on board the vessel are determined to be Haitian economic migrants who have left Haiti illegally and are heading for the U.S. they are transferred to the Coast Guard cutter and provided with food and emergency medical care. The migrant vessel is sunk for "reasons of security of general navigation." The Haitians are then returned to Port-Au-Prince, the capital of Haiti, and turned over to officials of the Haitian government, the Haitian Red Cross and the Department of State Returnee Officer.*** The Na-

---

*   Ibid.

**   According to a staff report on a study mission to Haiti, Haitian Migrant Interdiction Operation, Bill Woodward, Subcommittee on Coast Guard and Navigation (January 1982) as well as reports by interdictees.

*** Injustice on the High Seas: U.S. Interdiction of Haitian Boat People, op.cit.

tional Coalition for Haitian Refugees (NCHR) has received no reports of recent jailings or beatings of Boat People returned by the Coast Guard. However, refugees intercepted by Haitian authorities have reported many such instances during the Duvalier regime. Although their fate is largely unknown, the NCHR was able to obtain reports of people being jailed for the crime of leaving Haiti illegally.*

The U.S. government claims that the Haitians interdicted have not been endangered upon return according to inquiries undertaken by the American Embassy in Port-Au-Prince. Due to the limited nature of these inquiries regarding both the scope and the period of time when they were carried out, however, little value can be attributed to this statement.**

Interdiction circumvents both national and international legal prohibitions against refoulement, i.e., the expulsion or return of a refugee to a country where his/her life or freedom would be threatened. The Interdiction Program against Haitians is also sharply at odds with inspection and inquiry procedures that are regularly used with other groups of asylum seekers. These procedures provide an alien with the right to present his/her case to an immigration judge with the assistance of counsel.

Other Deterrence Practices

INS Treatment of Central American Asylum Seekers

Anna from Guatemala described her entry into the United States:***
> I left Guatemala with my husband and son because of the situation in my country and because I was a member of the

---

*   Ibid.

** The inquiries cover part of 1983. According to a "Status report on follow-up program on returnees and interdictees," less than 30 percent of the Haitians interdicted during that period of time have been interviewed. Some could not be located. Allegedly all of those interviewed asserted that they had not experienced any problems with the authorities since their return to Haiti.

*** These excerpts of her testimony are taken from The Underground Railroad, Renny Golden and Michael McConnell, Orbis Books, Maryknoll, N.Y. 10545, April 1986.

Catholic Church. I worked for the FENACOP (National Federation of Cooperatives) whose purpose is to serve the people and teach the poor how to read and write. One day, the government tried to kidnap me. That was when I decided to leave my country.

With her baby on her back, she tried to enter the United States illegally at the border of Nogales, Arizona. She was apprehended by INS agents and detained in a small room with just a chair where she had to sit all night with the child in her arms. When they interrogated her, she did not answer the questions, refused to sign deportation papers, and insisted on having access to counsel and a hearing before an immigration judge. The fact that she knew and insisted on her rights infuriated them, she said. She was not allowed to make a phone call and told that in the United States all those rights were not for women. Later, she was taken back to Nogales, Mexico, before a Mexican immigration judge who told the INS agents that she was Guatemalan. At that point, Anna was convinced that the U.S. agents were ready to leave her in Mexico and let the Mexicans deport her to Guatemala. In her desperation she made them swear that they, as representatives of the U.S. government, were forcing her to leave and insisted on having a hearing with the assistance of counsel.

Subsequently, she was taken back to Arizona to fill out some documents and detained in the same small room. She had been detained in Nogales for thirty-two hours without anything to eat and under stress:

> After a while, the door opened and a man wearing a drab, olive green uniform came in. He looked Central American. He shouted at me, "Listen, you fuckin' bitch, you're going to speak up right now. Who do you think you are? Who's advising you? Your parents in the church, right?" I was very scared because the situation reminded me of what was happening in Guatemala. There were moments when I thought he was going to torture me. He insulted me by calling me names that were very gross. He asked me where I was from and what my name was. I did not respond to anything because I knew any information would endanger my family and others back home. He pointed his fingers at me in a menacing way and said, "Look, you're not going to trick me. I'm a Central American." I told him that I wanted to see an immigration judge and that I al-

ready had a lawyer.

Finally the immigration agents took her out of the room and assured her that she was going to have a hearing with a judge. They took eight pictures of her, but when they filed them, one was missing. The Central American who had threatened her took it. Then in Guatemala it appeared on television; the announcer gave her name saying that she was a university student who had traveled to Cuba and accused her of being a guerrilla. He also offered a reward for turning her in to a security officer.

Anna concluded her testimony by saying: "That is why I can't return to my country."

Anna's account confirms widespread INS practice according to numerous testimonies of Central Americans. Many asylum seekers who manage to reach the United States have been denied a fair opportunity to present their claims. This has mainly affected Salvadorans, Haitians and Guatemalans who are generally considered by the INS to be economic migrants in search of a better life.

In April 1988, the Los Angeles Federal District Court decided the class action suit of *Orantes-Hernandez,* * brought on behalf of Salvadorans who have been or will be taken into INS custody, against the Attorney General and the INS. After having heard numerous witnesses testify on the treatment to which they had been subjected by the INS, the Court found that the INS had systematically coerced Salvadorans into not exercising their right to apply for asylum in the U.S. and ordered the INS to stop coercing Salvadorans who may have political asylum claims to return to El Salvador. The U.S. government has appealed.

The decision, which refugee advocates consider a landmark, includes factual findings about the human rights situation in El Salvador and the treatment of Salvadoran asylum seekers by the INS. In its factual findings, the Court states among a number of other things:

> A substantial number of Salvadorans who flee El Salvador possess a well-founded fear of persecution pursuant to United

---

* U.S. District Court of California in Orantes-Hernandez v. Meese and INS, CV 82-1107 KN, April 1988.

States asylum laws and the Refugee Act of 1980. People from a wide cross-section of Salvadoran society suffer human rights abuses. Trade unionists, members of farmwork unions and cooperatives, religious workers, human rights activists, refugee relief workers, members of student or political organizations, people suspected of opposition to the government or of being sympathetic to the opposition, family members and associates of those have been particularly subject to abuses.*

According to the court, INS officials process detained Salvadorans and other Central Americans by interrogating them and presenting them with a "Request for Voluntary Departure" form. A number of coercive practices are frequently employed by the INS, such as intimidation, threats, the misrepresentation of political asylum and the failure to give correct and complete legal advice. For this reason, most of the Salvadorans apprehended sign voluntary departure agreements and are immediately removed from the United States "even when they had unequivocally expressed a fear of returning to El Salvador."** The court also stated that the INS does not try to identify Salvadorans who might have a well-founded fear of persecution, nor does it notify them of the right to apply for political asylum. The INS frequently transfers Salvadorans, in particular, from the place of arrest to detention centers located in remote and isolated areas."***

These practices are outrageous in their aims to deny asylum seekers a fair hearing and adequate legal representation. They conflict with basic national and international obligations that have been established in order to protect refugees: the prohibition against returning them to a country where their life or freedom would be threatened; their constitutional right to due process; and their statutory right to apply for political asylum and withholding of deportation or exclusion.

---

*   Ibid., at 4.

**   Ibid., at 11.

***   Ibid., at 26.

In January 1989, another class action lawsuit was brought against the INS challenging newly-adopted policies and practices in the Western INS region regarding the adjudication of asylum applications and related employment authorization requests. The largely Central American plaintiffs, represented by seven refugee advocacy groups based in Los Angeles and the American Civil Liberties Union, claim that their class is routinely subjected to superficial and cursory interviews, to a total lack of confidentiality, and to examination without adequate interpretation or translation by examiners who are untrained or insufficiently trained in asylum law. Moreover, within the framework of a special "task force" instituted by the INS in the Los Angeles District, INS agents from other districts with no experience or inadequate experience in aslyum law have been assigned to Los Angeles to speed up the processing of asylum applications and employment authorization requests leading to a further deterioration in the conduct of asylum proceedings.*

New INS Policy Towards Central American Asylum Seekers**

On December 16, 1988, the INS introduced a policy of travel restrictions directed against Central Americans coming to the United States illegally, most of whom seek political asylum. The policy is aimed at preventing asylum seekers arriving in the Rio Grande Valley, in the district of Harlingen in southern Texas, from leaving the area until their applications are processed. Until then, they had been granted permission to travel to other areas, such as Los Angeles and Miami, where relatives and friends supported them while their cases were pending, and to pursue further their applications for asylum there.

This policy of travel restriction was challenged by immigration lawyers in a lawsuit leading to a temporary restraining order against the INS on January 9, 1989. The judge issuing the order explained that the INS would be allowed to

---

*   Mendez v. INS, United States District Court for the Central District of California, First Amended Complaint for Declaratory and Injunctive Relief, January 30, 1989.

**   The New York Times, January 7, 1989, "Suit attacks policy that keeps aliens in Texas," and January 11, 1989, "Aliens flee border area while rules are lifted"; and The Guardian, New York City, January 18, 1989, "Refugees face detention and squalor in Texas," and March 1, 1989, "INS clamps down on Central American Refugees."

reimpose the restriction as long as the refugees' food and shelter needs were provided for. Subsequently the order was vacated by the court, explaining that it "prohibits the functions and operations of an agency of the Federal Government" and rejecting the charge that the INS had violated its own procedures in the way it adopted the policy. The policy went into effect again.

On February 20, 1989, one day after the INS was allowed to begin enforcing the travel restriction policy, INS Commissioner Alan C. Nelson announced plans to begin detaining and deporting Central Americans in the Rio Grande Valley who are deemed to be economic rather than political refugees. According to the new policy, the INS may adjudicate affirmative asylum petitions in one-day hearings and detain the applicants immediately after their claims have been rejected at least until they can come before an immigration judge under deportation proceedings and ask to post bond. If they are not able to post bond, ranging on an average between $1,000 and $4,000 according to the INS, and unless they leave the country voluntarily, they will be in detention for weeks, perhaps months, if they choose to pursue appeals. Previously, they remained free while their appeals were pending. Refugees taken into custody by the Border Patrol before having presented asylum claims will also be detained. Previously, they used to be released on their own recognizance. The measures only apply to the southern Rio Grande Valley of Texas where most Central Americans enter the U.S.

According to INS officials, the new policy is designed to halt a dramatic increase of what the Bush administration considers frivolous claims for political asylum by Nicaraguans, Salvadorans, Guatemalans and other Central Americans. The INS argues that it is necessary to keep Central Americans from applying for political asylum, when they are, in fact, fleeing poverty. The INS maintains that these people are abusing the political asylum system. In a press conference, INS Commissioner Alan C. Nelson claimed that it was a "firm, fair and consistent application" of U.S. laws that:

> will meet the latest challenge of asylum abuse as a technique for fraudulent manipulation by those who would twist our generosity into personal gain.

The new policy is inhumane, unjust and not adequate to address the complex problems that cause mass influxes of asylum seekers. It denies Central American asylum seekers a fair hearing with guarantees of due process. According to Proyecto Libertad, one of the few organizations in the area providing free legal services to refugees, some 250 applications of Central Americans were processed on the first day of the implementation of the new policy. Of these applications, all but two -- both Nicaraguans -- were denied and the applicants were put in detention. Several of them reported that their interviews had lasted only 15 minutes; and that their adjudicators did not speak Spanish and apparently had no background in either asylum examination or evaluating country conditions in Central America. The number of applications dropped sharply the following two days, first to 30 and then to 12.

The majority of the applicants cannot obtain representation by counsel because few lawyers in the area practice immigration law. The speed-up of the process endangers genuine refugees by considerably increasing the likelihood of incorrect decisions. Deportation of refugees may violate the non-refoulement principle. The new policy's aim to deter Central Americans from applying for political asylum violates their right to do so, according to the Refugee Act. It also discriminates against Central American asylum seekers and violates the U.N. Protocol Relating to the Status of Refugees which prohibits imposition of unneccessary penalties or restrictions on refugees, irrespective of the manner of their arrival.

The Federal Government allocated considerable financial and personnel resources in the area in order to carry out the new policy. More than 500 federal officials have been mobilized, 269 of whom were assigned to the Border Patrol. To speed up the refugee determination process State Department officials have been stationed at the detention center.*

Since the district of Harlingen in Texas, where the Rio Grande Valley is located, is among the poorest in the U.S., it has not been able to accommodate the hundreds of people who were left stranded and homeless by the new policy. As of early January 1989, about 300 Central Americans were camping in a tent

---

*   Refugee Reports, February 28, 1989, "South Texas Detention Plan Goes Forward."

city with no sanitary facilities outside a church-sponsored refugee center. About 150 people were living in an abandoned motel with no windows, heat or plumbing. The refugee processing center in Harlingen was temporarily closed by local officials for violations of sanitary and fire laws. In mid-February 1989, processing of Central Americans was transferred to the remote detention center of Bayview, some 25 miles from Brownsville, far away from any means of public transport, grocery store or restaurant. Reportedly, asylum seekers walking there are arrested on their way and thus prevented from applying for asylum affirmatively.

The INS has erected a tent city with a capacity of 5,000 at the site of the Port Isabel Service Processing Center (PISPC) with a capacity of 1,100.* As of early March 1989, some 2,500 Central Americans were being held in detention at this site pending completion of their deportation hearings. Until early April, there was less than one telephone for every hundred detainees, a situation that effectively barred them from obtaining legal representation.** According to the INS, as of May 10, 1989, the number of detainees at the PISPC had dropped to 1,360 due to the expedition of the process and the highly increased deportation enforcement activities. According to the INS, as of May 10, 1989, 1,624 persons, mainly from El Salvador, Guatemala and Honduras, had been deported since the introduction of the new policy on February 21, 1989. Only Nicaraguans are for the time being exempted from deportation.

The new policy also abruptly reversed former Administration policies concerning Nicaraguans who had been invited by the Attorney General in the

---

* The New York Times, February 21, 1989, "U.S. set to detain refugees in tents beginning today."

** The federal district court of California stipulated in its decision in Orantes-Hernandez v. INS that there be at least one telephone for every 25 detainees.

summer of 1987,* which subsequently led to the fact that the number of primarily Nicaraguan but also other Central American refugees entering the United States increased considerably.

The fear that the INS will deport them to their homelands in keeping with the new tight regulations has driven Central American asylum seekers back to Mexico increasing the social burden of the country that has to live with an austerity budget.**

On April 28, 1989, Los Angeles Federal District Judge David Kenyon ordered the INS to stop deporting Salvadorans who have not been informed of their rights. The judge made this decision upon claims by refugee advocates that the new policy in Texas violated his order in *Orantes-Hernandez* regarding access to lawyers and access to legal information. According to Proyecto Libertad, the judge acknowledged that "the INS, in its blind zeal to deport people, had been breaking the law and the Constitution."***

Biases Due to Foreign Policy Interests

Rosa, a citizen from El Salvador,**** entered the United States without inspection on February 11, 1987, and was subsequently placed under deportation proceedings. In the course of the proceedings, she applied for asylum. She based her claim on the following personal account:

> In 1981, my brother was shot by a group of twelve men dressed in civilian clothing while responding to their summons. The men then proceeded to the bedroom where my common-law husband, myself and our three children were sleeping. They

---

* After the U.S. Supreme Court had liberalized the standard for refugee determination in March 1987.

** The New York Times, March 5, 1989, "Latin Refugees Are Fleeing Texas For Safer Haven With Mexicans." See also the section on "Discretionary Denial of Asylum" on Mexico as a safe haven for Central American refugees.

*** The Guardian, May 17, 1989, "Judge Accuses INS of Lying, Breaking Law."

**** File provided by South Side Community Annex, Immigration and Refugee Service, Brooklyn, N.Y. 11211. The person's name was changed in order not to endanger relatives back in El Salvador.

shot my husband leaving a note saying "FPL" "No Funeral." He was the *mayordomo* of the sugar cane section of the hacienda. Each of the twelve men then raped me while two others held me down. Each time one of them screamed, the child was beaten. After the men had left, I went with my children to the home of my father where we stayed for approximately six months. We then fled to the Department of Libertad where my mother and friends lived. We stayed there until around July of 1986. Since we had not heard of additional slayings and believed that the situation had somewhat improved, we returned to the Hacienda where we lived again with my father.

In late 1986, a group of men came to my father's home and requested that "the senora open the door." Since I was the only woman in the house I concluded that they were looking for me. We did not open. The men returned one week later and threatened to bomb the house, unless the senora opened the door. I fled after this incident to Nejapa and prepared to go to the United States.

In and around 1983, the *mayordomo* of the coffee section of our hacienda and his wife were shot. I heard the shots at about 10 p.m. and saw the bodies the next morning at 6 a.m. which also bore the note "FPL." In and around 1984, the *mayordomo* of our hacienda who replaced my husband was killed. The letters F.P.L. were carved into his face.

In the course of the hearing, the immigration judge expressed surprise about the fact that the death squads had killed the woman's brother and husband, but had spared her. He expressed the opinion that her claim of fear must be based on psychological problems, since nothing had happened to her since the first incident. He failed to take into consideration the incidents in 1986. He refused to hear the testimony of an expert witness who was present at the hearing on human rights conditions in El Salvador and rejected evidence relating to the killings of the *mayordomo* of the coffee section and his wife in 1983 for reasons not in accordance with INS regulations.

In his oral decision denying the asylum application, the immigration judge did not refer to any of the extensive evidence that had been presented in support of the personal account, but basically stated that the applicant had failed to establish a well-founded fear of persecution.

Although this individual case may be extreme, it illustrates widespread negative presumptions and biases held especially by district directors, but often also by immigration judges with an INS background, towards asylum seekers from countries with governments friendly to the U.S. government. Asylum seekers from such countries have a much lower approval rate than those from countries that are considered to be hostile towards the U.S., even when their claims are based on descriptions of the same incidents, such as torture, arrest, and life threats. In fiscal year 1988, for instance, the approval rate for Salvadorans was 3 percent and for Guatemalans 5 percent, as opposed to 77 percent for Ethiopians, 75 percent for Iranians, 53.7 percent for Poles and 53 percent for Nicaraguans.*

According to the study of the General Accounting Office (GAO),** those who described torture to support their asylum request had an approval rate of 4 percent from El Salvador, 15 percent from Nicaragua, 64 percent from Iran and 80 percent from Poland. The study concluded that the level of proof required seems to depend on the asylum seeker's country of origin. This corresponds to a 1982 draft INS internal report which noted that "different levels of proof are required of different asylum applicants."

But not only are asylum seekers from certain countries required to meet a higher level of evidence, they also seem to have to establish a higher level of persecution. Gang rape in the Salvadoran woman's case, and murder of her husband, weigh less in the balance than political imprisonment in the case of an East European and sometimes even less than denial of employment for political reasons.

Haitians, Salvadorans and Guatemalans have been special targets of negative presumptions. According to the experience of numerous immigration attorneys, asylum applicants from these countries face enormous difficulties when seeking to demonstrate a well-founded fear of persecution. Many INS dis-

---

*   Immigration and Naturalization Service/Department of Justice..

**   See the section on "Applying With an Immigration Judge."

trict directors, and immigration judges with an INS background, presume that aliens from these countries are economic migrants in search of a better life, while considering those from communist-dominated countries to be subject to persecution due to the nature of the political system. Poles and Afghans, for example, have the sympathy of the U.S. Administration and are, therefore, usually given the benefit of the doubt* by the INS as far as the determination of their asylee status is concerned.** Haitians, Guatemalans and Salvadorans, however, relating similar or even more terrible experiences, are likely to be found lacking sufficient evidence and credibility. Even when immigration judges accept their credibility, these applicants are frequently turned down because they have failed to prove that they face persecution throughout their homelands.

Work Authorization

The right to be granted work authorization is a crucial part of the statutory right to apply for asylum. Given the fact that asylum proceedings may well take more than a year, it is indispensable for asylum applicants to have an opportunity to earn a living. The INS policy to restrict increasingly this opportunity is of even more concern since the introduction of the Immigration and Reform Control Act in 1986 has made it virtually impossible for aliens to find illegal employment.

According to INS regulations, asylum seekers are to be granted work authorization within 60 days if their applications are considered to be non-frivolous. If the INS fails to adjudicate employment authorization requests within the mandated time, the applicant is entitled to obtain interim employment authorization.

Immigration officials determine whether an asylum application is non-frivolous solely on the basis of the application itself and the written arguments

---

*   As recommended by the UNHCR Handbook on Procedures and Criteria for Determining Refugee Status.

**   As far as Afghans are concerned, the INS used, however, to deny asylum to them as a matter of discretion because of circumvention of the orderly refugee admission procedure. The more liberal decision by the BIA in Matter of Pula might lead to significant changes in this INS practice.

of the INS trial attorney against the claim. Similar problems arise in this context as in the adjudication process. Biases within the INS are responsible for arbitrary and inconsistent practices regarding the granting and extension of work permits. In most parts of the country, few asylum seekers from El Salvador and Guatemala may obtain work permission while their cases are pending. Nicaraguans, on the other hand, were guaranteed approval of their requests for work authorization by an order of the Attorney General to the INS in July 1987.*

According to accounts of immigration lawyers both in the Western and Eastern INS region, the INS routinely fails to adjudicate employment authorization requests within the time mandated by regulation and, since a work permit is generally valid only for a period of six months, routinely fails to renew work permits for the period when the decision is pending on appeal with the BIA for reasons not in accordance with INS regulations. A New York City immigration attorney told Helsinki Watch that, on November 30, 1988, she submitted a letter to the Assistant District Director for Deportation in New York giving him the names and dates of employment renewal requests of 13 aliens beginning as early as May 1988. By mid-March 1989, she had only received responses for two.

The same official told an attorney that no work permit will be granted in a case on appeal with the BIA unless it is demonstrated in the notice of appeal that the immigration judge clearly violated the law. Asked to confirm this in writing he has not responded so far. However, the attorney has received denials of requests for extension of work permits for cases pending with the BIA on these grounds. Since this is not required by the INS regulations, it clearly demonstrates the INS's restrictive approach to granting work permits.

While such restrictive practices were not in the past offical INS policy, the INS recently announced that it would limit the possibilities for asylum seekers of any nationality to be granted work permits. The applicants will be required to present *prima facie* evidence of their claims, which is considered to be more burdensome than the non-frivolous standard.

In determining whether an application is non-frivolous, district direc-

---

*　　Refugee Reports, August 14, 1987, "Nicaraguans Hopeful, Waiting, Following Attorney General's Announcement."

tors and deportation officers should not rely on pre-conceived notions. Instead, they should give the applicants the benefit of the doubt; especially since the basis for evaluating non-fraudulence is a superficial one.

Right to Counsel

The right to counsel is an essential part of the right to due process, which is guaranteed to aliens by the U.S. Constitution. In order to enable asylum seekers to exercise their right to counsel, it is essential to provide them with full and correct information about free legal services.

According to the Lawyers Committee for Human Rights, more than 50 percent of all asylum applicants are not represented by counsel in proceedings with a district director. In immigration courts a large percentage are not represented. There is a right to counsel of choice, but the majority of all asylum seekers cannot afford to pay a lawyer; therefore, they are dependent on free legal aid. The INS distributes legal services lists, in accordance with its obligation to inform asylum seekers of the availability of free legal service programs through non-profit organizations. These lists, however, often contain inaccurate, incorrect or incomplete information.* Moreover, the INS has located its major detention facilities in communities where little or no legal representation is available to indigent detainees. The INS also routinely fails to notify attorneys that their clients have been transferred.**

---

*   U.S. District Court of California in <u>Orantes-Hernandez v. Meese and INS</u>, CV 82-1107 KN, April 1988, at 21.

** <u>Ibid</u>.

The Role of the State Department Advisory Opinions

Maria Teresa Tula* from El Salvador was a leading member of the Committee of Mothers and Relatives of Political Prisoners, Disappeared and Killed of El Salvador (COMADRES).** After having fled to Mexico in August 1982 to escape persecution by the Salvadoran Security Forces, she returned to El Salvador in October 1984. On May 6, 1986, she was abducted by plainclothed armed men. During her three-day detention, her unidentified captors tortured and raped her. They mutilated her stomach in spite of the fact that she was seven months pregnant, and repeatedly interrogated her about the activities of the COMADRES. She was left in a park with a deep stomach wound. Government sources denied that any security forces had captured or held her.

Three weeks later, she was again abducted, by four armed men in plainclothes. This time the government responded to inquiries by stating that the Treasury Police had arrested her on "suspicion of belonging to terrorist groups." She was held incommunicado for 12 days of interrogation during which she was repeatedly beaten and subjected to psychological pressure. After this, she was sent to Ilopango women's prison. She was never shown a warrant nor formal charges that she had committed any crime and was never tried or convicted of any charges during her three month period of detention.

Maria Teresa Tula was released from prison in September 1986 at the order of President Duarte. At a press-conference held by the government on this occasion, she denounced the government by pointing out one of her torturers standing in the crowd. She left El Salvador for the United States in January 1987 and applied for political asylum with the INS. Her application was denied by the district director in May 1988, based on the State Department ad-

---

*   File provided by Claudia Slovinsky, Attorney at Law in New York City.

**   COMADRES was founded in 1977, at the urging of Archbishop Oscar Arnulfo Romero, by a group of Salvadoran women. They provided moral support for each other and became advocates for all victims of human rights abuses. In 1984, COMADRES was granted the Robert F. Kennedy Human Rights Award.

visory opinion, on grounds of lack of evidence that members of COMADRES are presently being persecuted by the government of El Salvador. Moreover, the District Director stated in his decision that the applicant is not eligible for asylum because she was one of the leaders of COMADRES that is affiliated with an organization connected to terrorism.

In reaching these conclusions, the district director disregarded the extensive evidence collected by independent human rights organizations and presented by the applicant to substantiate reports of killings, torture and other appalling forms of persecution of members of COMADRES by government linked armed forces. The district director did, however, not hesitate to base his decision on the State Department advisory opinion which contains serious allegations without providing any evidence to support them.

The Department of State stated in its advisory opinion among other things:

> Whether or not Ms. T. was tortured while detained we cannot establish with certainty. Note should be taken, however, that a plan of action developed by the guerrilla organization, the Farabundo Marti National Liberation Front (FMLN), which fell into government hands on April 27, 1987, instructed guerrilla activists to allege, if they have been detained, that they have been tortured....

> ...Credible evidence linking the COMADRES to the guerrillas is in the hands of the Salvadoran and the U.S. governments, and in the public domain..., there is a guerrilla war in process in El Salvador and Ms. T. is a prominent guerrilla activist.

> There is no evidence that peaceful activity of a leftist character would cause her to be at risk in El Salvador at the hands of rightist inclined assassins.... Defectors from the FMLN have confirmed that Ms. T., in particular, has worked on behalf of the FMLN....*

---

* It is worth noting that the "defectors from the FMLN" in this case, two women, also charged that the Roman Catholic Church of El Salvador and other religious denominations were working on behalf of the FMLN. Though a number of persons were arrested on the basis of the charges by these two women and though several were abused in detention, none was ever brought to trial.

These serious allegations, supported only by accusations of the Salvadoran government, which receives strong U.S. government backing, also place the applicant in grave danger if she were to be forcibly returned to her country.

> Blanca DeRosal, a citizen from Guatemala and mother of two small children, decided to join the Group for Mutual Support (GAM) after her husband Jorge Rosal had disappeared following his abduction by paramilitary squads in August 1983. GAM, a human rights group formed by the relatives of disappeared Guatemalans,* investigates the fate of missing family members and works for their release by staging peaceful protests in front of government buildings, meeting with and questioning government officials, and publishing advertisements in the local newspapers. Blanca joined GAM despite the fact that she was repeatedly threatened and kept under close surveillance by Army intelligence agents after her husband's kidnapping.
>
> In March and April 1985, after then head-of-state General Oscar Mejia Victores had publicly denounced the GAM as "subversive" and had warned the group against "overextending the authorities' patience," two of the six leading members of GAM were assassinated, one of them along with her baby and 21-year-old brother. In May 1985, following the murders of her colleagues and threats against her own life, Blanca DeRosal, who had also been one of the leading members of GAM, fled to the United States with her two babies where she subsequently applied for political asylum.

In August 1986, the district director informed Blanca DeRosal of his intention to deny her application on the basis of the advisory opinion delivered by the Bureau for Human Rights and Humanitarian Affairs (BHRHA) which found that she had failed to establish a well-founded fear of persecution. The opinion pointed out that:

> During 1983 and 1985, she visited the American Embassy

---

* More than 40,000 Guatemalans have reportedly disappeared during the past decade after they were taken into custody by the armed forces.

several times for talks with the human rights officer about the disappearance of her husband, whom we have reason to believe was a member of a Guatemalan insurgent group....

In none of our meetings did she evince a concern for her personal safety. Rather, her focus was on the whereabouts of her husband.

The opinion focused at great length on a number of statements attributed to Blanca DeRosal that allegedly demonstrate that she did not leave Guatemala because of fear for her and her children's life and safety. While giving great weight to other persons' statements about her alleged lack of fear (even counting against her the fact that she focused on the fate of her husband rather than on her own situation in a conversation with Embassy personnel prior to the assassination of her colleagues in the GAM), the BHRHA failed to give appropriate weight to Rosal's own expression of fear which the incidents of murder and threat strongly support. The Department of State also argued that the advent of an elected civilian government "committed to human rights improvements" indicated that she would be safe from persecution if forced to return.

The State Department's arguments were clearly designed to support the U.S. government's decision to back the newly-elected government. It failed to evaluate adequately the applicant's individual situation. Despite the fact that Blanca DeRosal had been persecuted in the past, the Department of State based its opinion in her case on vague assumptions and expectations of future improvements of the general human rights situation that contradict findings of independent human rights organizations.

Given the fact that those Guatemalans who are labelled guerrillas and their family members are frequently threatened, summarily executed and "disappeared" by the armed forces, the State Department's statement linking Blanca DeRosal's husband to Guatemalan insurgent forces is particularly irresponsible since it fails to provide any evidence to support this serious allegation. He had been the proprietor of a small business and had never been accused of any crime before he was abducted and disappeared. Most likely, this statement constitutes a repetition of an allegation originating from the Guatemalan military and reflects a retroactive effort to justify what happened to him. It further endangered the Rosal family if forced to return to Guatemala.

Though Blanca DeRosal was one of the lucky few who eventually obtained asylum despite an advisory opinion by the Bureau for Human Rights and Humanitarian Affairs opposing asylum, her case, along with Maria Teresa Tula's, clearly illustrate the nature of the State Department advisory opinions and their role within the asylum determination process. Since the Bureau for Human Rights and Humanitarian Affairs of the State Department in charge of preparing the advisory opinions does not use sources independent of friendly governments in evaluating the situation in the country of origin of asylum applicants, the advisory opinions closely conform to U.S. foreign policy considerations causing bias, inconsistency and lack of credibility of the U.S. asylum procedure.

The State Department opinions are supposed to be merely advisory, but, in fact, according to the study carried out by the General Accounting Office (GAO), there are few instances on record in which a district director has countered State Department directives. Opinions delivered by the BHRHA are actually decisive of the outcome of the vast majority of the cases decided by district directors. Ninety-five percent of the Department of Justice's decisions on asylum applications conform with the Department of State's advisory opinions. In the case of differing decisions, INS examiners are likely to change their preliminary decisions in accordance with the State Department's view.

The size of the special asylum staff at the BHRHA is not sufficient to process the enormous number of asylum requests. Neither the staff in the asylum section, nor those in the regional offices who prepare the advisory letters, are specially-trained to handle problems related to evaluating asylum claims and, therefore, lack qualifications adequately to take into account the particularly complex nature of asylum claims.

Each staff member handles the cases of a geographic region, e.g., Asia, the Middle East, Latin America. BHRHA staff members complete most of the opinions based on the applications themselves and their own experience with similar cases. On cases the staff considers difficult or controversial, the BHRHA official may ask for corroborating information from the country desk officer of the asylum applicant's country of origin, or even from officials in the

U.S. Embassy in that country.* Many advisory opinions are form letters, either recommending approval or denial without adequate explanation and documentation of the sources of the information, or the basis on which the recommendation was made. Under the new detention and deportation policies in south Texas, State Department personnel even started merely to append yellow stickers onto the application forms stating that the Department lacked specific information on the applicant and referring to the human rights reports of the Bureau for Human Rights and Humanitarian Affairs on the countries of origin.**

The importance that is attached to these opinions and the failure to involve an independent agency, such as the UNHCR, in at least an advisory function in the asylum determination process are major weaknesses of the entire asylum system.

---

*　See: "Applying for Political Asylum in New York: Law, Policy and Administrative Practice," Patricia Weiss Fagen, April 1984.

**　Refugee Reports, March 17, 1989, "House Hearing Examines U.S. Asylum Policy Options."

THE NEED FOR TEMPORARY PROTECTION

There are entire groups of aliens who, although they cannot establish that they meet the narrow refugee criteria, would be in danger if they were returned to their countries, and thus are in need of temporary refuge in the United States. As of now they are without any meaningful protection. The passage of the Immigration Reform and Control Act (IRCA) of 1986 has created an even greater need for protection of those aliens in refugee-like situations. Since the Act imposed severe penalties on employers who hire, recruit or continue to employ unauthorized aliens, it has deprived them of any means for earning a living in the United States. Prior to the passage of the IRCA, this group of aliens enjoyed at least some protection due to weak attempts to pursue their deportation.

Aliens of certain nationalities have been granted Extended Voluntary Departure (EVD), a temporary relief which has evolved through INS practice since 1960 as a merely discretionary, extra-statutory measure. It is a temporary non-deportation status granted at the discretion of the Attorney General to citizens of a certain country who, whether or not they individually meet the refugee criteria, would face persecution and life-threatening situations if forced to return to their country. These situations can be conditions of civil war or various forms of pervasive violence. EVD may also be granted to individuals on a case-by-case basis.

No national group, still in its own country, in whatever serious situation it may find itself, is entitled to EVD. A State Department memorandum from 1983 states that EVD is granted, usually upon recommendation of the State Department, to aliens physically present in the U.S. It is based upon an overall assessment of the U.S. national interest, including foreign policy, immigration policy, and humanitarian issues. Thus, the Executive branch, through the office of the Attorney General, has the sole discretion to determine what groups will be granted EVD status. It does so upon determination by State Department officials that conditions in the countries of origin are unstable or unsettled or show a pattern of "denial of rights." There is no provision for systematic consultation with Congress. The Attorney General's decisions are not considered to be subject to judicial review. This has led to inconsistencies and arbitrariness in granting this remedy.

The federal government has granted the status unevenly, favoring those nationality groups with whom the United States shares an ideological interest. During the past, this status has been granted to 16 nationality groups, including Cubans, Czechs, Chileans, Hungarians, Romanians, Ugandans, Nicaraguans, and Iranians. It is presently in effect for Afghans, Ethiopians who arrived prior to June 30, 1980, and Poles.* It may also be granted to Lebanese on a case-by-case basis.

Because of the ongoing violence, human rights groups have been urging the U.S. government to grant EVD status to Salvadorans in the United States fleeing violent conditions in their country. Since the U.S. Administration supports the present Salvadoran government, the State Department and the INS have refused, giving priority to foreign policy considerations over the needs of Salvadorans. Curiously enough, the former Salvadoran president Jose Napoleon Duarte asked the U.S. government not to send Salvadorans whose applications for asylum have been denied back to El Salvador because, in his opinion, they are likely to support the guerrilla movement.**

The "Moakley-DeConcini Bill," which would preclude detention and deportation both for Salvadorans and Nicaraguans for two years following enactment, pending a study on human rights conditions in both countries, as well as the "Temporary Safe Haven Act" died with the end of the Congressional term in 1988, but both are expected to be reintroduced in the new Congress.

---

*   "A Preliminary Discussion of Considerations in Enacting Temporary Refuge Legislation," Lawyers Committee for Human Rights, July 1987.

** The New York Times, September 11, 1988, "Salvadoran Issues a Refugee Appeal."

The "Temporary Safe Haven Act" addresses the need for a temporary grant of protection to any national group of persons in a refugee-like situation. It would provide authorization to nationals of certain countries in crises* to remain temporarily in the United States, until the conditions in their country of origin have improved sufficiently to allow their safe return. During this period, they would be authorized to work. The Act would ensure that the stay of these aliens would be temporary by obliging them to register with the government. They would then be issued temporary documentation, valid for 18 months, which would render them ineligible for permanent residence status.

While the proposed legislation addresses an important need in an efficient way, it does not contain adequate provisions to narrow the Attorney General's discretion in determining the countries to be granted the relief, a fact that is mainly responsible for the inconsistency and arbitrariness of the present system.

---

* The crises in the countries are either an ongoing armed conflict, an environmental disaster or humanitarian, international or immigration concerns.

APPENDICES

Overall Statistics Regarding Asylum Cases Filed with U.S. District directors*

	number of applications**	granted	denied	rate of approval
1981	61,568	1,175	3.346	25 %
1982	33,296	3,909	7,255	35 %
1983	26,091	7,215	16,811	30 %
1984	24,295	8,278	32,344	20 %
1985	16,622	4,585	14,172	24 %
1986	18,889	3,359	7,882	30 %
1987	26,107	4,062	3,454***	
1988	60,736	5,531	8,582	39 %

Statistics by Selected Nationalities

	number of applications	number of approvals	decisions denials	appr.rate
1984				
Afghanistan	153	186	269	40 %
Cuba	3,401	16	472	3 %
El Salvador	5,455	328	13,045	2 %
Ethiopia	415	305	1,014	23 %
Guatemala	510	3	758	0.3 %
Haiti	2,163	23	352	6 %
Hungary	78	62	160	27 %
Iran	3,488	5,017	3,216	60 %
Nicaragua	4,807	1,018	7,274	12 %
Poland	852	721	1,482	32 %

---

* Source: Immigration and Naturalization Service (INS)/U.S. Department of State.

** An application may include the applicant's spouse and children under 21.

*** Note: This figure does not reflect substantial numbers of drafted denials which were not completed prior to the end of FY 87 due to clerical shortage.

1985
Afghanistan	173	57	188	23 %
Cuba	2,684	61	565	9 %
El Salvador	1,661	74	2,299	3 %
Ethiopia	420	187	387	32 %
Guatemala	313	5	427	1 %
Haiti	631	4	670	0.6 %
Hungary	64	46	66	42 %
Iran	2,734	2,779	2,400	53 %
Nicaragua	5,025	408	557	8.5 %
Poland	976	451	737	37 %

1986
Afghanistan	195	48	63	43 %
Cuba	3,043	17	649	2 %
El Salvador	2,183	55	1,149	4.5 %
Ethiopia	391	175	202	46 %
Guatemala	471	5	209	2 %
Haiti	176	2	514	0.3 %
Hungary	105	22	24	47 %
Iran	2,236	1,172	828	58 %
Nicaragua	7,111	1,082	2,873	27 %
Poland	965	373	376	50 %

1987
Afghanistan	102	22	62	26 %
Cuba	3,684	70	110	38 %
El Salvador	2,684	29	776	3.6 %
Ethiopia	519	165	184	47 %
Guatemala	640	7	178	3.8 %
Haiti	75	0	69	0 %
Hungary	116	14	56	20 %
Iran	1,675	967	468	67 %
Nicaragua	13,377	1,867	357	84 %
Poland	1,284	447	497	47 %

1988
Afghanistan	110	36	55	39.5 %
Cuba	1,683	30	64	31.9 %
El Salvador	27,048	110	3,822	3 %
Ethiopia	900	441	131	77 %
Guatemala	6,384	24	447	5 %
Haiti	314	6	13	31.5 %
Hungary	212	24	59	28.9 %
Iran	1,742	764	254	75 %
Nicaragua	16,170	2,786	2,455	53 %
Poland	2,487	433	373	53.7 %

Ceilings on Refugee Admissions and Actual Refugee Admissions to the United States (FY 1981 to 1988)*

	1981	1982	1983	1984
Total				
ceilings	217,000	140,000	90,000	72,000
applications	193,230	94,769	104,190	107,437
approvals	155,291	61,527	73,645	77,932
denials	15,322	14,943	20,255	16,220
appr.rate	91 %	80 %	78 %	82 %

	1985	1986	1987	1988
ceilings	70,000	67,000	70,000	83,500
applic.	93,415	81,017	101,718	
approvals	59,436	52,081	61,529	70,874
denials	18,430	9,679	13,911	10,785
appr.rate	76 %	84 %	81 %	87 %

	1984	1985	1986	1987	1988
Africa					
ceilings	2,750	3,000	3,500	3,500	3,000
applic.	6,570	4,539	3,671	4,395	
approv.	2,743	1,943	1,329	1,974	882
denials	1,906	1,585	877	892	429
appr.rate	59%	55%	60%	69%	65%
Asia					
ceilings	52,000	50,000	45,500	40,500	47,000
applic.	79,502	64,397	54,591	67,693	
approv.	64,116	45,626	41,190	47,166	38,707
denials	10,125	13,753	6,501	10,665	5,012
appr.rate	89%	77%	86%	81%	89%
Eastern Europe Soviet Union					
ceilings	11,000	10,000	9,500	10,000	30,000
applic.	21,033	22,348	22,644	29,278	
approv.	10,917	9,999	9,515	12,290	23,517
denial	4,059	2,924	2,294	2,305	3,037
appr.rate	73%	77%	80%	84%	82.5%

* Source: Immigration and Naturalization Service (INS)/U.S. Department of State

Latin America					
ceilings	1,000	3,000	3,000	4,000	3,500
applic.	332	2,131	111	352	
approv.	156	1,868	47	99	1,705
denials	130	168	7	49	320
appr.rate	54%	92%	87%	66%	84%

	Poland	Kampuchea	Vietnam	Iran	Ethiopia
1984					
applic.	9,647	26,545	31,040	12,725	6,025
approv.	4,288	21,444	28,875	5,419	2,536
denials	2,241	5,099	2,120	1,503	1,674
appr.rate	65%	80%	93%	72%	60%
1985					
applic.	9,365	21,563	25,038	6,819	4,134
approv.	3,001	11,380	23,799	3,496	1,771
denials	1,321	10,181	1,203	804	1,554
appr.rate	69%	52%	94%	81%	53%
1986					
applic.	10,581	2,996	31,040	8,799	3,141
approv.	3,734	2,084	28,975	3,231	1,285
denials	1,156	4,490	1,396	1,229	784
appr.rate	76%	69%	93%	72%	62%
1987					
applic.	11,971	1,800	21,429	13,919	3,858
approv.	3,568	1,187	18,362	6,658	1,808
denials	1,384	604	2,920	1,230	868
appr.rate	72%	66%	86%	84%	67%
1988					
approv.	2,532	3,916	19,692	4,347	833
denials	2,337	1,467	3,046	1,647	425
appr.rate	52%	73%	87%	73%	66%

SOURCES

- Aleinikoff, Alexander T., "United States Immigration, Nationality and Refugee Law" in *The Legal Position of Aliens in National and International Law,* Jochen Abr. Frowein/Torsten Stein, Springer Verlag 1987.

- Immigration and Nationality Act of 1952 as amended by the 1980 Refugee Act, Pub. No. 96-212, 94 Stat. 103.

- Immigration and Naturalization Service, *Worldwide Guidelines for Overseas Refugee Processing,* August 1983.

- Interpreter Releases/Report and Analysis of Immigration and Nationality Law, Federal Publications Inc, September 21, 1987 and April 11, 1988.

- Helton, Arthur C., *Manual on Representing Asylum Applicants,* Lawyers Committee for Human Rights, December 1984.

- Helton, Arthur C., "Political Asylum under the 1980 Refugee Act: An Unfulfilled Promise," Mich. Journal of Law Reform, Winter 1984.

- Helton, Arthur C., "The Legality of Detaining Refugees in the United States," Review of Law and Social Change, New York University, Volume XIV, 1986.

- Human Rights Watch, Lawyers Committee for Human Rights, "Refugee, Asylum and Immigration Policy" in *The Reagan Administration's Record on Human Rights in 1988,* January 1989.

- Lawyers Committee for Human Rights, Helsinki Watch, *Mother of Exiles/Refugees Imprisoned in America,* 1986.

- Lawyers Committee for Human Rights, *A Preliminary Discussion of Considerations in Enacting Temporary Refuge Legislation*, July 1987.

- Refugee Policy Group, *Political Asylum: A Background Paper on Concepts, Procedures and Problems,* Washington D.C., December 1982.

- U.S. Committee for Refugees, *Despite a Generous Spirit: Denying Asylum in the United States,* December 1986.

- U.S. Committee for Refugees, "Refugee Reports," Washington D.C.

- U.S. Department of Justice/Immigration and Naturalization Service (INS), statistics on asylum cases filed with district directors and refugee-status applications.

- U.S. General Accounting Office, Study on the Practices and Procedures of the Department of Justice and Department of State in Judging Applications for Asylum in the United States, January 1987.

- Weiss Fagen, Patricia, *Applying for Political Asylum in New York: Law, Policy and Administrative Practice,* April 1984.

Copies of this report are available for $7.00 from:

HUMAN RIGHTS WATCH

485 Fifth Avenue
New York, NY 10017
212-972-8400

1522 K St., NW
Room 910
Washington, D.C. 20036
202-371-6592

in Europe:

**INTERNATIONAL HELSINKI FEDERATION
FOR HUMAN RIGHTS**

Rummelhardtgasse 2/18

A-1090 Vienna, Austria

43-1-42-73-87

ASYLUM SEEKERS IN THE UNITED STATES

Although the right of asylum is not yet acknowledged by the international community to be one of the basic human rights, the need for it stems from a lack of respect by governments for internationally-recognized human rights. The states where people seek refuge have a moral and legal obligation at least to grant them refuge by not sending them back to the country where their lives or freedom were threatened.

Helsinki Watch advocates the continuation of a generous and humane asylum and refugee policy by the United States towards all nationalities. By examining U.S. law, recent administrative and jurisdictional developments in the refugee determination process, and policies that have been heavily criticized by refugee advocacy groups, this report seeks to raise public awareness of recent threats to the system of refugee protection in the United States and to enlist public support for a better system.

June 1989
ISBN 0-929692-22-5